YES, YOU CAN

Build Deeper Relationships,
Earn More Money and
Be a Happier You!

Elizabeth Lucas-Afolalu

10-10-10
Publishing

Jacqueline Irenäus
Amazing Lady
Thank you

YES, YOU CAN
Build Deeper Relationships,
Earn More Money and
Be A Happier You!

ISBN: 9781791541637

Published by:
10-10-10 Publishing
Markham, Ontario, Canada

Table of Contents

FOREWORD

Would you like to achieve more success and happiness in your life? Author Elizabeth Lucas-Afolalu believes that, if you explore your uniquely feminine values and refuse to compromise, you will be able to change your mindset about how to achieve that success and happiness.

You are about to make new decisions and new choices. There will be no fear-induced limitations, but instead you will begin to work towards succeeding and improving yourself and your relationships, and staying happy in the process. In the pages of this book, you will learn how to be an overcomer, how to manage yourself, how to relate effectively personally and professionally, and how to turn negative situations into positive ones.

By being truthful to yourself and others, you will find *huge* power and success.

Raymond Aaron
New York Times Bestselling Author

ACKNOWLEDGEMENTS

My gratitude to Almighty God, who has given me this assignment and opportunity to share and write this book: YES, YOU CAN.

My gratitude also goes to:

My mentors, family, friends, and well-wishers who have motivated me to write, and those people who have educated me through their books, audio, and other resources.

My first mentor, Mrs. Florence Adesoga, for her inspiration and wisdom. She gave me my first lesson in love and a relationship, stood by me during my wedding ceremony, and continues to support me today. She opened her home to me to observe and to learn, and I saw how women should behave, even in the midst of storms.

My Pastor, Matthew Ashimolowo, for his tireless teaching, which has challenged and motivated me to be the best in everything I do, and to never settle for less.

Andy Harrington, whose Power to Achieve event transformed and empowered me to look on the inside and to never be afraid to start a new chapter in life, and to share my story with the world.

Les Brown, TD Jakes, Oprah Winfrey, and Lisa Nichol, for inspiring me to keep going on with this project.

My business and marketing coach, Larry Palmer, for his constant advice, support, and inspiration.

My outstanding coach, Chinmai Swamy, for his regular recommendations and inspiration, as well as for his time and effort in reading my book.

Raymond Aaron, and the team, who have helped to make this long-term dream come true.

My loving and caring husband, and my wonderful children, for their permission to use them as my platform for experiencing and exhibiting love. Thanks to them also for their support in writing this book.

All my friends and relatives, who have supported me on my long journey to experience, learn, and grow stronger.

Also, you, the reader, for trusting me to inspire you to start believing that YES, YOU CAN, and that all things are possible.

DEDICATION

I dedicate this book to:
All women, young adults, and married couples.
Those who are seeking to build deeper relationships, make
more money, and be happier.
My darling husband and wonderful children.

AFFIRMATION 1

Yes, I can do it.
Yes, I can have it.
Yes, I can be it.
Yes, I can achieve it.
Yes, I can complete it.
Yes, I can perfect it.
Yes, I can finish it.
Yes, I can relate.
Yes, I can be empowered.
Yes, I can develop.
Yes, I can succeed.
Yes, I can create wealth.
Yes, I can do it.
Yes, I can change.
Yes, I can adapt to change.
Yes, I can become.
Yes, I can marry.
Yes, I can be fulfilled.
Yes, I can go after what I want and get it.
Yes, I can take up anything and improve it.
Yes, I can take any situation, turn it around,
and make it work for me.
For all things work together for good to them that believe;
so say it, believe it, and it shall become real.

CHAPTER 1

YES, YOU CAN HAVE NEW AND BETTER BEGINNINGS

I have some important questions to ask you:

- Do you think you could become, be, and do much more than you are now?
- Do you need motivation and help to develop perseverance to pursue your life goals?
- Do you want to develop the mind-set that will push you to improve your character traits that will lead you to unlimited success in life?

Many people continue to carry their negative past experiences with them in the journey of life, and have lived lives marked with negativity and mediocrity. A life that is full of "I CAN'T," while afraid to step out of their comfort zone and out of poor self-confidence and low self-esteem. This has been affecting several personal and professional lives today.

The most successful and the happiest people in the world always work to improve themselves, to be better than they were yesterday, and it is this constant work on personal growth that brings them closer to their life goals every day. Nothing will change unless you change; nothing will get better unless you get better. If you want change, then you make that change. The body has its limitations, but the mind is not limited. The attitude and lifestyle of constant personal discovery and growth requires a specific mindset that wants to learn and work on personal development, and will awaken in you the drive to discover more and to do more. This book will help you to acquire this mindset with ease, and in the most natural way possible. When you renew your mindset, then your life can be transformed and free, and you can be happy.

For so many years, the statement of "YOU CAN'T" followed me everywhere. I heard it from family, friends, relatives, co-workers, colleagues, teachers, lecturers, managers, and trainers. However, God, the Creator, who created ME, has proven them wrong!

Yes, YOU CAN do this...it is not easy, but it is POSSIBLE. Start by believing God and, very soon, you will believe in yourself.

Based on what people have said to us, or said into our lives, we say to ourselves, "I have no talent;" "I'm not creative;" "I cannot do it;" "I'm too old;" "I'm too young;" "I'm too tired;" "I'm too busy;" "People won't let me;" "I'm afraid;" "People don't believe in me;" etc.

> *"Sometimes the people you love the most turn out to be the people you can trust the least."*
> Trent Shelton

There is TIME out of no time, and we need to create it. There are different ways to do things. You can do what you want to do, what you enjoy doing or love doing, and you can leave the rest for others to do. We cannot do everything. There are many gifts in you, and when they are recognised, can benefit the whole world, and the Bible says that the gift in you will make room for you. This means that the gifts within you can create great opportunities for you when you discover them. Therefore, create the time for your dream to manifest. Time does not wait for anybody. To transform your life to greatness, your mindset first has to be renewed. For your mind to be renewed, you've got to study thoroughly. For example, reading books, listening to audios, and watching videos that are transformational and motivational.

Finally, work on your beliefs. What do you believe about yourself and your situation? Do you believe the worst about every situation, or are you a positive person? Help yourself to develop a positive mindset. Then put your positive thoughts into action by going after and doing what you need to do to accomplish your goals. The Bible says, "Faith without works is dead." This means that believing only achieves results when you *do* what needs to be done. Faith is what gives substance to things hoped for, things not yet seen. Faith is the opposite of fear, and you can develop faith through reading and listening to faith building materials.

NEW WAYS OF THINKING IF YOU WANT TO BE HAPPY IN LIFE

The mind is amazing and is a powerhouse. The mind is used for acquiring knowledge. You can conceive and achieve with your mind. Your mind can be a doorway or barrier to your destiny, depending on how you think, for you become what you think about. It is your thoughts that helped shape your boundaries. Your mind is a producer of your present circumstance. Therefore, arise, conquer through right thinking, and achieve.

You have to think right if you want to build more meaningful relationships, earn more money, and be a happier you.

Our thinking must be constructive, productive, creative, inventive, and positive. Be progressive in your thinking. Progressive thought will lead you to discover new wisdom. You will keep growing while you are thinking.

Think constructively. Get fresh insight on a new thing. It will help you to see the future and show you the solution. You will discover what you need to know. If it is going to be, then it is up to you. Expand your horizon. Read books, listen to audios, attend seminars, and watch videos that are relevant. Ensure you have within your network those that help you to think right, to grow and to achieve.

"Finally, brethren, whatsoever things are true, whatsoever things are honourable, whatsoever things are just, whatsoever things are pure, whatsoever things are lovely, whatsoever things are of good report; if there be any virtue, and if there be any praise, think on these things."
Philippians 4:8

LOOK INSIDE

In life, we were taught to look outside ourselves for all the things we thought were missing from our lives, but the truth is that there is a life-force within each person. Look inside and discover yourself. Your heart and soul are a lot wiser than you think, and if you could just get into the habit of conversing with your soul—listening, trusting the one that created us—you will soon discover that all the answers you were once so desperately seeking outside yourself, are within you when you converse with your creator. You are more valuable than all the labels that have been placed on you. You are neither a finished product nor a fixed being. Who you are is constantly changing, growing, and developing. You will become new and better every day.

You should not wait for others to validate your self-worth. It is a truth that other people cannot determine how worthy and valuable you truly are. Most people have no idea how valuable they themselves are. Most people allow external things, places, people, and circumstances to determine how much they are worth, and so they judge you as being worthy or not so worthy, based on the same criteria. You should know that these things have nothing to do with your value and self-worth. Don't fall into the trap of thinking that whom you are is not enough, and that you need other people's approval, love, and validation in order for you to feel worthy or valuable. Never allow external things, places, people, or circumstances to determine how much you're worth, and there is no need to compare or compete with anyone or anything else. The life you are meant to create, and the person you were born to be, are unique. You are unique right from when you were created, and since your path in life is different from everybody else's, there is no need to compare or compete with anyone or anything else.

NEXT CHAPTER

In my next chapter, I will share my own personal experience on how I have turned the opinions of others around and how I didn't allow people's opinions to disturb, distract, or limit me. I have shared this in order to inspire my fellow women and younger ones across the globe. You can achieve, you can have deeper relationships, and be happy. Don't allow people to discourage you; most of them don't know what you are capable of or who you are. You are bigger than the situation you are facing right now. Come with me to the next chapter as I share and unveil my true story of how I turned the voice of negativity into possibility, and how I have believed in myself and was able to rise above other people's opinions in order to make things happen for me, despite the odds. All things are possible when you believe.

CHAPTER 2

YES, YOU CAN TURN THE NEGATIVITY OF OTHERS INTO POSSIBILITY

It was time to sit for GCSE examinations, but I was not trusted to do well at all. My parents underestimated me and felt that I could never pass the examination, and that the registration money for such an exam could be put to better use; so my parents refused to pay for my registration for the exams. However, by divine intervention, I still sat for the GCSE examinations. When the results came out, I visited one of my teachers, who was also my mentor. After dinner with the family, she called me aside and told me that my results were not good enough for me to further my studies, and she then gave me the parable of the snail and the bat.

In that story, both creatures set out for their journey. The bat got to his destiny quickly enough, while the snail also got to his destiny eventually, while taking his time slowly. Both of them got there in the end. She explained that some people would achieve success in their career smoothly and quickly—for example, go from secondary school straight to university, and start work immediately after graduation—while some will need to go through other forms of training to achieve career success (e.g. being an apprentice). However, at the end, everyone will be fulfilled and be successful. So, she encouraged me that the result was not the end of the journey, or the end of the road for me, and that I would still succeed. Mrs. Shine was the only teacher, and the only person, in Nigeria, whoever spoke positively into my life before I came to the United Kingdom. Despite many disappointments, including when my desire for further training did not materialise, and Dream Helpers, who could have helped me, were discouraged from doing so, I held on to the inspiring words of Mrs. Shine.

One day, I had a dream that I was celebrating my success and wearing a graduation gown, standing in front of people and delivering a message on a platform with great people. I said to myself, when I woke up, that it was not possible. I even thought that perhaps it was my choir gown I had seen myself wearing in that dream, since I was a chorister and Praise Worship leader in a local church and school.

At some point in time, some couple felt they should help me to go back to secondary school so as to retake the GCSE exam. I was so happy, and I rushed off quickly to share the good news with my parents. Unfortunately, they rejected this plan and offer, and I was denied this opportunity. I was asked to look for a job instead. I was unemployed for so many years until I started secretarial training and worked for a couple of months as Courier Secretary at Fenway Limited. Then, an opportunity came for me to travel to the United Kingdom.

When I came to the United Kingdom, in 1988, I met all kinds of people, including my relatives, who said it wasn't easy or possible to fulfil any dreams in this kind of environment. They said I could not continue working as a secretary and that I could not even work in an office environment in this country. They undervalued and underestimated what I could do. They encouraged me to just look for cleaning or menial jobs to survive. They also said it was difficult to get Council accommodation and that I could manage with them in their own apartment. They also said I would need to lie and compromise to get an accommodation from the Council. So, I found myself again back to square one, working hard and working all kinds of cleaning jobs and sales assistant jobs, night and day. I struggled and continued living an average and mediocre life. I even served successfully as a maid, cooking, doing all the domestic work, and still paying rent and being denied freedom and the benefits of a British citizen who was born in England.

DECISION MAKING

I decided it was time to move forward and to pursue my dreams and goals. First, I decided to move away from the negative environment in which all I was told was how impossible my dreams and goals were. I sought help from the Council for accommodation so as to change my location and to move away from negativity. I completed the application for a Council flat honestly and without compromise, and God granted my request—it was a big surprise when the Council offered me a council flat so quickly. With gratitude to God, I was able to show kindness and generosity to accommodate other female relations and friends who found themselves challenged and stranded in England, and I accommodated and helped them.

I met a man of God who challenged me, saying, "Young lady, you are unique, and there is greatness in you, and no matter your background and what you have been through and your present position, United Kingdom is a place of opportunities, which you can embrace, and where you can develop yourself." He continued, "So, don't settle for less; don't settle for second best, and don't settle for average. Your gift, potential, personality, and character will help you and open doors for you. Career or no career, you will make it and be successful."

I developed interest in Creative Entrepreneurship and, coupled with my secretarial skills, I was always looking for adventures of success. With the encouragement and motivation I received, I kept pressing on. I had now developed computer skills and administrative skills, as well as my secretarial skills. I also did all kinds of trainings and had become very creative. During my studies, an English teacher once told me that I would never pass the assessments, and this was as I was working hard on my studies while nursing my two little children. Guess what? I passed the NVQ 3 in Administration, and RSA computer skills, and the college and Brook Bureau awarded me *Secretary of the Year*.

My first job was at the Local Government Management Board, as a word processing and desktop publishing administrator, where I helped with updating the examination question papers for the Fire Brigade and the Defence. Some years later, I progressed to Tower Hamlet Consortium as the receptionist and desktop administrator. Here, I met the director of the company, who was so kind to me and saw great potential in me, and so gave me the opportunity to work flexible hours so I could take care of my young children. I was even able to attend more training to boost my confidence, and I gained better computer skills and graphic skills.

At some point, it was necessary to step back and support the wonderful children that God has blessed me with, and I became a full-time mother and housewife to my wonderful family. During that time, I also acted on the message of my pastor, which encouraged each person to still do something tangible in every situation, and to create a job that accommodates your present situation if you are not able to find one that does. With that attitude, I started a business endeavour—selling gifts, cards, and stationery in the market—and I eventually started creative and inspirational writing. I now had a gift shop, which enabled me to have the time to see to the wellbeing of my children and my husband. I was able to get involved in various activities in my children's school, and I even became School Governor of Childeric Primary School, in New Cross, London, for many years. I worked hard and bought two properties. I moved to a better place and a better environment, and my children went to a better school, which was one of the top graded schools in the United Kingdom, where they developed their skills, talent, and passion.

I went back to work in the office, at Salvation Army, a homeless Christian charity, for many years, and then trained in customer service. Both my supervisor and manager had both said I was not capable of achieving success on that course, but I proved them wrong and finished the course with distinction. This led me to become a leader in that career.

NOT ALLOWING THE SITUATION TO STOP OR LIMIT ME

Situations and circumstances will make you stronger, even if it feels difficult, as it might sometimes be. It could be a great opportunity for you to succeed. There was a time when something terrible happened. I had an emotional and mental breakdown. I was depressed and became suicidal. Again, I reminded myself not to let the situation defeat me or stop me. I reasoned that what did not kill me would only make me stronger. I had health problems for almost a year, which caused me to be hospitalised. I also suffered haemorrhaging for six months. While still on treatment, I had a minor stroke. However, I recovered quickly. During that time that I could not work but could only concentrate on getting well, I encouraged myself with the "It is not over until you win," "All things are possible," and "YOU CAN" motivational messages of my pastor. I believed all these and, once again, I made up my mind to press on and to be proof of "I CAN." Of course, there were still some dream killers who tried to discourage me, as they focused on my circumstances. However, there were encouragers too. I am grateful to my children and my husband, who believed in me and encouraged me to achieve my dreams. I believed that I could do all things through Christ who gives me strength to do it.

PROGRESS

During the time of my recovery from stroke, I then decided to develop myself again. I studied HNC and HND Business and Marketing. Again, a lead lecturer, who taught me communication and decision making, felt I could not do well in those subjects. She downgraded me and avoided supporting me while I was studying my HND, but I also proved her wrong, as I graduated with merit and distinction. This lecturer was so pleased that she then encouraged me to progress to a university degree course. I attended the University of Northampton, where I achieved a 2:1 honours degree in business and management. Initially, I had experienced health problems again, and had to have an operation, but I did not let that stop me. Another lecturer, my dissertation supervisor, became doubtful and threatened to downgrade my work, but later became the first person to break the good news of my success to me by congratulating me by email. This is to prove that if you set your mind to do something, no one can stop you. I did it, and if I could, then YOU CAN. It is possible.

I worked hard in various organisations as secretary, administrator, and personal assistant to directors, as well as high judges and district judges in Central Family Court, until I became CEO/director of my own companies. I am still striving to succeed higher. Success is an ongoing thing, and I cannot stop striving until I close my eyes to sleep in glory. So, YOU CAN do this...it is not easy, but it is POSSIBLE. I became an inspirational writer, speaker, and coach. I became director of Tokmez Limited, and managing director of Elizabeth Kreations. I am also a relationship and family mentor, along with my husband. In 2017, I became the UK Bureau Chief Editor of an American magazine called *Okuns Group Magazine*, where I contribute my inspiration columns.

IN THE NEXT CHAPTER

You can succeed in life with the 5D steps: Desire, Dreams, Determination, Discipline, and Decision. These are steps I have taken personally, which helped me in my journey of life, especially during the difficult times. I am using this next chapter to inspire you that if I could, YOU CAN, and that it is possible.

CHAPTER 3

YES, YOU CAN SUCCEED IN LIFE WITH 5D STEPS

The 5D steps are Desire, Dream, Decision, Determination, and Diligence.

DESIRE

Have you been in this sticky situation before? Where you've had a burning desire to pursue a life-long passion but couldn't—because you were stuck in a career that society, your parents, your family, or your education expected you to pursue? You're not alone. Countless people find themselves sacrificing their passions for a more *reasonable* or *practical* path in life. But is there a way you can make a *course correction,* and steer your life back towards those passions that once captivated your imagination as a child? I was privileged to mentor and support my daughter with her choice of career. I gained a lot during that period. As her parents, we had wanted her to study medicine because it was our desire for her to become a medical doctor, and we felt she had the ability to do so too. She is so brilliant and creative. We went through a series of counselling. She maintained her reasons for not wanting to study medicine and gave reasons why she chose the career that she chose. We had to respect her decision and to understand her point of view that it's her happiness and fulfilment in her career that is of vital importance. Her desire in this matter is of more importance than ours. I am hoping to use this experience to encourage and coach other parents as they support their children with their career choices.

What we desire in life is usually an indication of our passion, our dreams, and our goals and aspirations.

DREAM

I had a dream, a wonderful dream, but I was too broke to implement it, too tiny to do it, and too small to accomplish it. I've been there too many times! Life was tough. Opportunities passed me by, just because I was a NOBODY. People wanted my products and not me! It was tough, because I was not famous. I was not rich, and I was not *connected*. It was rough. Doors were shut left and right, and I had no helper. I noticed people were stealing my glory and crushing my hopes. I tried several times, and yet nothing happened. Several times, I did odd jobs just to survive. Nevertheless, I kept dreaming, even when my hopes were crushing, I kept dreaming. Even when they turned me away, I kept dreaming. Even when they shut me down, I kept dreaming. No one knows what you are capable of except yourself! People may judge you by how you look or by what you have. But please, fight on! Fight for your place in history. Fight for your glory, and never quit and never give up. When there is life, there is still hope. Keep up the fight. Keep your dreams and hopes alive. Go great. Yes, YOU CAN, when you take action—when you put to action what you believe. Set a goal for your dream.

"A goal properly set is halfway reached."
– Zig Ziglar

"Goals are the fuel in the furnace of achievement."
– Brian Tracy

DECISION

Once you have a desire to achieve a goal, you have to make a decision to do what it takes to achieve it. From my illustration earlier, my daughter made a decision regarding her career choice. As I mentor others, I advise them to research the pros and cons, advantages and disadvantages, and also effects or consequences of each option before making a decision. It is the same in personal life or career as it is in business. You need to research and analyse findings.

DETERMINATION

Once the decision is made, then you need to determine that you will succeed and work hard. The level of your passion and desire for the project will be the level of your determination. Determine that you will not quit or give up. In my coaching sessions and mentoring, I help each person to set up the strategy to sustain growth and to push forward in all areas of life. Determination is very important. Let us determine to succeed in our personal relationships, in our career, and in business. Let us be determined to find a solution to any problem rather than quitting or running away.

In my coaching sessions, I help individuals set goals and create strategic plans to achieve their goals. Goal setting is an important secret to success in any area of life. However, setting a goal may seem simple, but it is not so easy to achieve those goals. It takes courage and hard work to achieve goals because you will need to overcome obstacles and challenges. However, there are time-tested methods that will help you get the success you dream of. Knowing exactly what your goal is and being willing to pay the price to achieve it is key to success. Success is mostly as a result of dedicated planning and effort. Focusing on your goal every day, being passionate about it, and taking consistent action will help you in achieving your goals quicker.

DILIGENCE

Why pursue diligence? It qualifies you as a leader. You were called to stand out and be distinguished. Whatever you do, do it diligently. If it is encouragement you have been called to do, then do it diligently. If it is giving, then give generously. If it is to lead, do so diligently. If it is to show mercy, do it cheerfully (Roman 12:8). Excel in whatever you do so that you can be effective. Diligence qualifies you for service; it multiplies God's grace to you; it exposes the gifts and talent in you, and it will help you fulfil your dreams. Diligence requires discipline— discipline in integrity, in honesty, in hard-work, and in commitment. We can define self-discipline as self-control, self-government, or self-restraint. Discipline is orderliness, good behaviour, routine, or regimen that produces desired results and helps you to demonstrate diligence.

Love and enjoy what you do. That love will see you through difficult times. Be yourself and manage your time well. Don't be afraid to make mistakes. Hold yourself accountable. Learn from your mistakes and grow—grow stronger, better, and wiser. You should spend time thinking about how to do better in future. Remember, you want to do better. This will help you stay focused, disciplined, and diligent during tough times.

Fruitfulness or getting results is a characteristic of being diligent. There will be abundance and increase. The diligent person will be disciplined and work with what they have, and will go the extra mile. They will choose their companions carefully. They will pursue their goals and take bold action that will require faith.

NEXT CHAPTER

I discovered that 80% of what we are afraid of never does happen. Fear is a force that can potentially influence just about anything a person does. If you can start to look beyond your fear, you may find that the FEAR is just False Evidence Appearing Real. In the next chapter, be encouraged to step up the game, deal with fear, and open your eyes to see the opportunities around you.

CHAPTER 4

YES, YOU CAN BE FREE FROM FEAR AND TURN FEAR INTO OPPORTUNITY

THE ELEPHANT ROPE

As a man was passing by the elephants, he suddenly stopped, confused by the fact that these huge creatures were being held by only a small rope tied to their front leg. No chains, no cages. It was obvious that the elephants could, at any time, break away from their bonds, but for some reason, they did not. He saw an elephant trainer nearby and asked why these animals just stood there and made no attempt to get away. "Well," the trainer said, "When they are very young and much smaller, we use the same size rope to tie them and, at that age, it's enough to hold them. As they grow up, they are conditioned to believe they cannot break away. They believe the rope can still hold them, so they never try to break free."

"Fear will only hold you down and limit you. Too many of us are not living our dreams because we are living our fears."
– Les Brown

Richard Branson said, *"If opportunity comes, take it first, and then figure it out."*

Recently, I became involved with an event called London for Jesus, organised by Jesus Fellowship; it was immediately after the Brexit referendum, where the United Kingdom decided to leave the

European Union. A bomb attack, carried out in another European country, brought a threat to the United Kingdom, and many people in Britain were afraid of a terrorist attack. Many people from different religions and community groups were gathered at Trafalgar Square.

During our event, some of us walked around to talk with people in anticipation of opportunities to bring words of hope and encouragement to them. We also prayed with them. However, people were afraid and uncertain about tomorrow. There was a feeling of hopelessness, and people were saddened, worrying about the future. Business was not as usual. Fear gripped many people. There were so many kinds of fears, such as fear of going out, especially to a public place, fear of terrorism, fear of whether to sell their property, fear of losing their jobs and being unemployed, fear of homelessness, fear of lack, and insecurity and fear of being in an isolated situation. It was because of that atmosphere that I decided to throw some light into the darkness and to write about overcoming fear, in order to lift people's spirits up and to inspire them.

The dictionary defines fear as an unpleasant emotion caused by the belief that someone or something is dangerous, likely to cause pain, or is a threat. Fear is a feeling of anxiety concerning the outcome of something or the safety and well-being of someone. Fear is what causes a person to put off doing something because that person is afraid.

THERE ARE TWO KINDS OF FEAR

There are two kinds of fear. There is the fear of God and the fear of man. The fear of God is a total acknowledgement of all that God is, and this comes through knowing Him and His attributes. Fear of God brings with it many blessings and benefits. It is the beginning of wisdom and leads to good understanding (Psalm 111:10). Only fools despise wisdom and discipline (Proverbs 1:7). Furthermore, fear of God leads to life, rest, peace, and contentment (Proverbs 19:23). It is the fountain of life (Proverbs 14:27) and provides security and a place of safety for us (Proverbs 14:26).

The second type of fear mentioned in the Bible is not beneficial at all. This is the *spirit of fear* mentioned in 2 Timothy 1:7 (NKJV): "For God has not given us a spirit of fear, but of power and of love and of a sound mind." A spirit of fearfulness and timidity does not come from God.

It is said, 80% of what you are afraid of never happens. Anxiety is usually wrapped up in anticipation of how things will or won't go. It is an emotion that looks to the future. Fear intimidates and limits our movement. It is the apprehension of evil. Fear empowers the adversary. Fear stops the flow of faith, and fear is a tormenting spirit. Fear is a spirit like a sickness. Also, fear is a tool of Satan and disturbs you from thinking (1 john 4:4). Fear can manifest as phobias, such as fear of public speaking, fear of animals, fear of heights, etc.

TURNING FEAR INTO POSITIVE ENERGY

You can turn fear into positive energy and use it to your advantage. For instance, many people experience stage fright, but the fear leading up to a performance can help you concentrate in that moment and focus intensely on what is before you. Learn to acknowledge the fear, and then direct it to where it will be most beneficial. Most people experience fear prior to an event, and yet experience no fear when in the middle of the situation. Remember, that fear heightens your senses so that you have the ability to perform efficiently and powerfully.

Fear can create a great opportunity. It can help to identify problems that need solving, like a red signal that is a warning when there could be danger or when something needs attention. It is the moment when one needs to examine and learn from the situation. When you feel fear of something unfamiliar, take it as a sign that you need to investigate the situation better before you commit to it. If you feel a flash of fear about an upcoming deadline or event, make it an opportunity to make a plan of action to get fully prepared; whatever you need to do to make sure that you are ready for that event or situation. Turning fear into positive energy also includes being vigilant, not being careless, taking the right level of precaution, watching out for others in your neighbourhood, etc.

AVOID BEING PARANOID

Do not give yourself a lot of time to wallow or sit around thinking about what everyone else is thinking or saying about you. Though staying busy can't help you escape your problems, it can help you focus your energies on more productive outlets, such as pursuing your interests or attaining your personal goals. If you spend even a few hours a week pursuing a hobby that you really love, you are guaranteed to be less absorbed in your paranoid thoughts. If you have anxiety, then you may be plagued by worry and a constant fear that something may go wrong. Anxiety may even trigger your paranoid thoughts, though these two conditions are different. For example, anxiety may cause you to worry that you're suffering from a fatal illness, but paranoia may lead you to believe that your doctor purposefully made you sick.

There's a difference between occasionally worrying that all of your friends are talking about you, and letting this thought completely consume you. There's also a difference between knowing that your thoughts are irrational on some level, and suffering from serious delusions that everyone is really out to hurt you. If you feel like your paranoid feelings are taking over your life and preventing you from enjoying your everyday interactions or socialising, then talk to a psychologist or other mental health professional to get help for your condition.

FOCUS ON WHAT YOU CAN CONTROL

Learn to focus on what you can actually control, while still engaging with what you cannot. For example, a person may be worried about whether they might develop heart disease, but there are certain factors that they cannot control about heart disease. Such factors as family history, race and ethnicity, and age. That person will make themself more anxious by focusing on those things. Instead, it's far healthier to focus on the things they can control, such as quitting smoking, exercising regularly, and eating well. In fact, a person is at higher risk of heart disease when they have an unhealthy lifestyle than by just the uncontrollable factors alone.

GUIDE YOUR LIFE

When we want to control the direction of our lives, we are often met with disappointment, frustration, and anxiety about things that don't go as planned. Learn to loosen your grip on how tightly you control the outcomes of your life. You can still make plans, of course. Guide the course of your life. But allow some room for the unexpected. A fitting analogy is the idea of water flowing in a river. Sometimes the riverbank will change, the river will curve, and the water will slow down or speed up. The river is still flowing, but you have to let it go where it takes you.

ELIMINATE UNPRODUCTIVE THOUGHT PATTERNS

When you try to predict or imagine the future, you find yourself asking, "What if this happens?" This is an unproductive thought pattern known as catastrophising. An unproductive thought pattern is a way of thinking about a situation that ultimately causes you to have negative emotions. How we interpret an event will result in the emotion we feel from it. For example, if you are worried that you're late for work, you might tell yourself, "If I'm late, I will get reprimanded by my boss, and I'll lose my job." Having unproductive thought patterns can put you on edge. Replace unproductive thinking with positive thinking. Reason through your unproductive thought patterns. For example, say to yourself, "If I'm late, my boss might get mad. But I can explain that there was more traffic than normal. I'll also offer to stay late after work to make up the lost time."

THINK ABOUT HOW YOU'RE AFFECTED BY OTHERS

When other people's worries start taking over your mind, you'll think more about risks too. Perhaps you have a friend who is particularly negative about diseases and illnesses. This causes you to feel nervous about getting ill yourself. Limit the time you spend with this person so that these thoughts don't enter into your head so frequently. Try something you've never done before. We often avoid trying new things and putting ourselves in new situations because of fears regarding what we do not yet know or cannot yet understand.

In order to practice letting go of control, pick an activity you had never considered doing, and commit to giving it a try. Start by doing some research on it online. Next, maybe talk to people who have participated in the activity before. As you start to become more comfortable with the idea of it, see if you can't give it a try once or twice before making an especially long commitment to it. This method of experimenting with life and new activities can be a great tool for learning how to focus on producing joy in life as opposed to worrying.

As you participate in new activities, you will likely learn a lot about yourself, especially in regards to what you can and cannot control. Spend time in nature. Go on meditative walks in nature. These activities can be great ways to become more comfortable with the realisation that you're a part of a larger world. Keep a gratitude journal. A gratitude journal is a way for you to write down and acknowledge the things you're thankful for. This will help keep your focus on the good things in your life. Think of good things about your life and cherish them. Take some time every few days to write down a moment or thing that you're grateful for. Write in depth, savouring the moment and appreciating the joy you've received from it. Spend time with your loved ones. Surround yourself with people that make you happy, and vice versa. Your time will be well spent, and well-remembered, when you share yourself with others.

It's impossible to think clearly when you're flooded with fear or anxiety. The first thing to do is take time out so you can physically calm down. Distract yourself from the worry for 15 minutes by walking around the block, making a cup of tea, or having a bath. If you start to get a faster heartbeat or sweating palms, the best thing is not to fight it. Stay where you are and simply feel the panic without trying to distract yourself. Place the palm of your hand on your stomach and breathe slowly and deeply. Avoiding fears only makes them scarier. Whatever your fear, if you face it, it should start to fade. If you panic one day getting into a lift, for example, it's best to get back into a lift the next day. Try imagining the worst thing that can happen—perhaps it's panicking and having a heart attack. Then try to think yourself into having a heart attack. It's just not possible. The fear will run away the more you chase it. It sometimes helps to challenge fearful thoughts. For example, if you're scared of getting trapped in a lift and suffocating, ask yourself if you have ever heard of this happening to someone. Ask yourself what you would say to a friend who had a similar fear.

DEALING WITH STRESS

Many of us feel that our lives must be perfect, but bad days and setbacks will always happen, and it's important to remember that life is messy. Take a moment to close your eyes and imagine a place of safety and calm. It could be a picture of you walking on a beautiful beach or snuggled up in bed with the cat next to you, or a happy memory from childhood. Let the positive feelings soothe you until you feel more relaxed. Sharing fears takes away a lot of their scariness. If you can't talk to a partner, friend, or family member, call a helpline, such as the Samaritans (116 123, open 24 hours a day). Lots of people turn to alcohol or drugs to self-treat anxiety, but this will only make matters worse. Simple, everyday things, like a good night's sleep, a wholesome meal, and a walk are often the best cures for anxiety, and give you a treat. When you've made that call you've been dreading, for example, reinforce your success by treating yourself to a massage, a country walk, a meal out, a book, a DVD, or whatever little gift makes you happy.

"For God gave us not a spirit of fearfulness; but of power and love and discipline." (2 Timothy 1:7). Fear will not stop your destiny. Fear will not stop your purpose. What you are afraid of will not destroy you. Fear will not hold you down; fear will not kill you. Fear will not limit you. You will rise to another level, and the promises of God will sustain you.

ARISE AND SHINE!

Your knock down is not a knock out. It is a setup for a lift up, and your setback will become a setup for lifting. God will turn the evil to good when you are looking unto Jesus, the author and finisher of our faith and the joy that has been set before us. Hard-pressed and not crushed, perplexed but not in despair, persecuted not forsaken, struck down but not destroyed, troubled but not distressed, fallen down several times but not totally cast down, for you shall rise again. When you stop under the tree of discouragement, when you hear evil reports, just understand that it may be the fact but not the truth. Just remember that our focus must be on the Lord. Get ready for your lift up, even when you think you have failed God. His mercies endure forever. He is faithful and just to forgive your sins, for there is therefore now no condemnation to them which are in Christ Jesus, who walk not after the flesh but after the Spirit. Remember, your past is not your future, God is not going to consult your past for your future, and His grace is sufficient. Remember, you are at the bus stop and not there permanently. You are going through but not stuck there. Despite all these things, you are more than a conqueror. God did not bring you this far to leave you. Never give up, for God has called you. Remember the call and the purpose; remember the companionship, for you are not alone. God is with you. He will not leave or forsake you. Remember the consolation that you will soon be rewarded.

NO CONDITION IS PERMANENT

The affliction is for a moment. These hard times are small potatoes when compared with the lavish celebration prepared for us. There is no glory without a story, no triumph without tribulations, and no testimony without testing. Let us rely on God's wisdom, strength, and grace. Remember the story of Job, Paul, and David in the Bible. Be encouraged, as it is stated of David in the Bible, "David encouraged himself" in the midst of the storm. Rise up and shine. When a situation throws you down, get up and remain standing. Be bold, be strong, for the Lord our God is with you. Greater is He that is in you than he that is in the world. Arise and shine again. Believe in yourself that you can do all things; take a step, take a giant leap. Yes, you can!

IN THE NEXT CHAPTER

I will discuss in the next chapter why change is needed for us to survive and thrive. We too have to start the change process. We sometimes need to get rid of the unpleasant old memories, negative habits, and our fixed mindset. Who cares what people know about your past? Your past is not your future. Instead, we have to update our knowledge and refresh our memories. We have to have a flexible approach to adapt to change. You can still start afresh; you can begin again—you can, and it is possible!

CHAPTER 5

YES, YOU CAN ADAPT TO CHANGE, BE MORE SUCCESSFUL AND EARN MORE MONEY

Today's opportunities are a way to erase the failure of yesterday. Failure does not mean you are a failure; it means you have not succeeded yet, and you need to do something differently next time. Failure does not mean you stop or quit but that change is required to improve and to get better results. Failure does not classify you as inferior, but it means you are not perfect and are willing to change for the better. Failure does not mean you have been disgraced; it only shows you are willing to try and that you will try a different way until you get the desired results. Failure does not mean you have accomplished nothing; it means you have learned something. Failure does not mean you have wasted your life; it means you have a reason to start again and embrace good change. Failure does not mean you have been a fool; it means you have a lot of faith and wisdom. You are born to achieve in life, and you will succeed.

Any challenge you are going through now will only make you stronger. Though you may feel broken and bruised now, you will recover from this ordeal a more resilient person. When we get injured, the scar tissue that develops to mend our damaged skin is stronger than you could ever imagine. It's the same for your heart and soul: trust in their ability to heal, too. In keeping with this, celebrate your failures as lessons learnt. As the wonderful Oprah Winfrey encourages, think like a king or queen. A king or queen is not afraid to fail. Failure is another step to greatness. Take heart and have faith in the fact that thanks to the experience, you will be better equipped to deal with whatever life throws at you next.

Let me share with you the story of an eagle. The eagle has the longest life span of its species. It can live up to 70 years, but to reach this age, the eagle must make a very difficult decision. In its 40th year, the eagle's long and flexible talons can no longer grab a prey, which serves as food. Its long and sharp beak becomes bent. Its old, heavy wings, due to their thick feathers, stick to its chest and make it difficult to fly. Then, the eagle is left with only two options: DIE or go through a painful process of CHANGE! This process lasts for 150 days (5 months), and the process requires the eagle to fly to a mountaintop and sit on its nest. There, the eagle knocks its beak against a rock until it plucks it out. Then the eagle will wait for the new beak to grow back, after which it will pluck out its talons. When its talons grow back, the eagle starts plucking its old feathers for new ones to grow. And after this, the eagle takes its famous flight of rebirth, and lives for 30 more years!

WHY IS CHANGE NEEDED?

Why do we need change in our lifestyle and in our relationships? In order to survive and thrive, we have to start the change process. We sometimes need to get rid of the unpleasant old memories, negative habits, and fixed negative mindset, and this is possible. How have you increased your skills, knowledge, abilities, or income in the past 90 days? Do you really expect to be successful given how you are using most of your time, resources, and skills, or do you realise that you need a good change in any of these areas? Are you spending time with people who can enhance and enrich your life? What are you doing to take your life to the next level? Will your current efforts make the next 90 days even more successful than you just experienced? Be honest with your assessment.

I believe anything worth doing takes courage. It takes courage to do something you know everyone won't love. It takes courage to keep going when people around you don't or can't understand. It takes courage to look them in the eye and say what you think. Negative relationships, negative emotions, and low self-esteem can hinder purpose. However, you know you need to show up and share why you are here. You need to embrace good change to fulfil your purpose. You may be scared, but do not remain mediocre; do not stay in your comfort zone, and do not live an isolated life without fulfilment.

If an eagle can make a life-saving and life changing decision at the age of 40, why can't we? In order to take on a new journey ahead, we need to let go of old, negative and limiting beliefs. Open up your mind, and let yourself fly high like an eagle! When it rains, all birds occupy shelter. But the eagle avoids the rain by flying above the clouds. Having a problem is common to all, but the attitude to solve it makes the difference! Don't be afraid of change...accept it gracefully! Arise and shine.

SHOW UP AND SHARE WHAT YOU'VE GOT FOR THE WORLD

Not showing up will hurt you and everyone else, because you help no one by hiding. If you don't do what you know is your purpose or vision to do, someone else will do it. If you don't work on your vision, then you will work on other people's vision. So, you need to build yourself and your abilities in order to contribute to solving the world's problems. It's really none of your business what someone thinks of you. If someone doesn't like what you are doing, it doesn't mean others don't.

Sometimes life just gets to be a little too much, and it's easy to get overwhelmed. Whether it is expectations from your boss, colleagues, friends, family, or other half, or even the sky-high expectations you have of yourself, occasionally, it all comes to a head, and you are left feeling like you are not good enough. Your mind can be cruel, so don't always take it at its word. We are often our very worst critics. Even if we are kind to others, it can be hard for us to be nice to ourselves. We tend to judge ourselves extremely harshly, whether we are aware of it or not, simply because we are conditioned by society to believe we need to look or behave in a certain way. In times like these, it can be difficult to gain the perspective you so need to pull yourself out of that terrible slump. No one can do better than you because there is not a single person out there who is like you! You are blessed with unique attributes that make comparing yourself to anyone else not only futile and discouraging but also, quite frankly, impossible. No one has lived the life you've lived, so no one is better equipped to tackle your challenges than you. Remember this whenever you catch your subconscious trying to convince you that you are not as worthy as someone else!

You are good enough to try, and that's all you need to do. Now that you know that failures should be celebrated and not feared, the time has come to realise that everything you've accomplished up until now, and everything you'll achieve henceforth, comes from you taking a leap of faith and trying. No matter how convinced you are that you are going to fail, make the attempt. It's the most important part of any endeavour, and the only one that is really asked of you. Progress trumps perfection always. It is so easy to get caught up in others' expectations that we forget that perfection is an unrealistic (and frankly, boring) ideal. By shooting for perfection, you are setting yourself up for feeling like crap when you inevitably fall short. Progress, on the other hand, is a better measure of how brilliant you are and how much you've grown. Celebrate every small step forward.

No need to be in a huge hurry. Just because everybody else is running ragged doesn't mean that you need to hold yourself to the same crazy standards. The greatest achievements in life take time to accomplish. So, no need to pressure yourself into getting everything done all at once when you can't quite manage it. Sometimes you need to surrender to your feelings and allow yourself to not be superwoman or superman for once. The world will carry on turning without you holding it together. Give yourself permission to give in to your emotions and know that it's okay to give yourself a break. You've worked so hard, you deserve it.

You are not alone. Although insecurity tends to confine us to a very lonely place, know that there are people around you who think you are amazing and that you matter.

We spend our lives bending over backwards trying to please others, trying to conform to others' ideals, and losing sight of what really matters, which is our happiness and our fulfilment. At the end of the day, people come and go, but you are stuck with yourself for the rest of your life. So, yours is the approval that really matters. Do yourself a favour and focus on how you feel about yourself before worrying about the others. I'll bet that once you strip away others' expectations, you'll like what you see. You have overcome so much already. You may feel terrible now, but remember how much you've already achieved. Think about the path that has led you to where you are now. Reminisce about your life from an objective perspective, and see how much you've accomplished and overcome. Though it may not seem like it now, you are a warrior, and you are capable of so much.

AN ATTITUDE OF GRATITUDE

There is so much to be thankful for. It is a great exercise for gaining a little perspective. Though things may seem like they are going wrong, being able to make a gratitude list reminds me that there is a silver lining. You may feel terrible about yourself now, but I can guarantee that there is so much beauty in you. In times when you don't feel good enough, try making a gratitude list...for yourself! Name three things that you love about yourself. Be as silly or as ceremonious as you like. If you are having trouble with coming up with something, be grateful for your lungs, which allow you to breathe; your mouth, which allows you to smile; and your soul, which makes you. You are a thing of wonder, and you should believe it!

RECOGNISING OPPORTUNITY

When things go wrong, as they sometimes will; when the road you are trudging seems all uphill; when the funds are low and the debts are high; when you want to smile but you have to sigh; when care is pressing you down, then take a bit of rest if you must, but don't you quit. Success is failure turned inside out. It may be near when it seems far, so stick to the fight when you are hardest hit. It is when things seem worst that you must not quit. There is no easy way to break through; there is no breakthrough without war; there is no victory without battle; there is no success without hard work; there is no increase without labour; and there is no testimony without tests and trials. So, therefore, expect opportunity, and search and look for opportunity, for great things are always hidden. Only diligent search leads to the greatest discovery. Where others see failure, you see success. Every day, you are surrounded with great opportunity. Look for it, and you will find it.

Everything you do not respect exits your life. Friends, contacts, relationships, and chance are all opportunities, and your attitude should be shown by the respect you give. Value opportunity, and don't lose it. Don't let ego push you out. Know the importance of the season and time. Recognise, value, and respect opportunity, and don't take things for granted.

TIME IS MONEY

It is very important to understand the value of time. It is true that if you don't plan and have a goal, you cannot value and appreciate time, for you will be going everywhere, anywhere, anytime, because you lack the ability to dedicate your time. Year after year, such people make new promises, which never come to fruition because they did not bother to dedicate the time required towards their goals. Time management skills, learning how to say no, and knowing what commitments to undertake, while avoiding procrastination, is a step towards great success in any area of our lives and relationships.

> *"Any successful entrepreneur knows that time is*
> *more valuable than money itself."*
> – Richard Branson

> *"The person who says it cannot be done*
> *should not interrupt the person doing it."*
> – Chinese proverb

Isn't it interesting that so many people who have never tried something are quick to tell you it can't be done? Now, most people are quick to dismiss an idea with the opinion that they could never do something like that, or that you wouldn't make any real money from it anyway.

> *"The best time to plant a tree was 20 years ago.*
> *The second-best time is now."*
> – Chinese proverb

So, go plant your *tree*, now!

YOU CAN EARN MORE MONEY AND MANAGE YOUR FINANCE EFECTIVELY

Managing our finance is a major factor that will boost our success in life. One of the statements I held on to is the fact that a person who knows and manages the little he has can be better than the one who has millions but does not manage it properly. This has been proven among wealthy people. What you do with little will reflect what you will do with a lot. Do not despise your small beginnings. Learn to spend money wisely. The first rule of spending money is that you spend only what you have and not what you expect to make, unless it's an emergency. This will keep you out of debt and planning well for the future. When you have a financial goal and implement it, it will make a massive difference in the future. I recommend that we should start to train our young ones, and they will rise up and become better in the way they deal with money and become successful. In my research, finance is one of the problems or challenges that families and relationships have faced.

PROFESSIONAL ADVICE

Once you are ready to grow your wealth and begin investing, you should speak to a financial planner to help you make your investment decisions. A good advisor will explain the risks involved in each investment, and help you find products that match your comfort level while helping you work towards your financial goals as quickly as possible. A financial planner can also help you with your budget, which is another plus. Remember that investing is a long-term strategy to building wealth. Also, ensure that you get advice and make good choices about insurance coverage, such as life Insurance, health insurance, home owner insurance, etc. Consider having an emergency fund and a retirement plan, as well as funds for the children's education. You can also find financial help elsewhere and find a mentor that would be willing to walk you through your budget in the first few months. This can help you if you are overwhelmed with your budget. If your parents or family members are good with money, consider asking them for help. Sit down and talk with them about what worked for them financially, and what they would have done differently.

IN THE NEXT CHAPTER

In the next chapter, I will unveil to you how I have personally overcome challenges and obstacles in all kinds of relationships, and how I have helped other individuals and families to grow and maintain deeper relationships. I discuss why family and relationships matter in life, and I share how I have turned my own personal relationship experiences to a learning curve, implementing what I call the *Imperfect Principles* in all areas of my life. I discuss how I have been able to build family relationships, working relationships, relationships with customers, and relationships within the business environment, within the society, and among leaders. There are many stages and principles that I have shared in this chapter that will benefit individuals and families.

CHAPTER 6

YES, YOU CAN RELATE

WISDOM FOR RELATIONSHIP

R   Recognise and celebrate your differences and similarities, and strengths and weaknesses
E   Endure, express yourself to one another, and encourage
L   Love and Listen
A   Acknowledge and appreciate, affirm and admit your mistakes
T   Trust
I   Identify potentials and gifts, and inspire one another
O   Observe and overcome obstacles
N   Nurture your love and relationship
S   Submit, sacrifice selflessly, and stay faithful
H   Have hope that things are going to get better, and believe it is possible
I   Integrity and honesty will help you build your trust for each other
P   Pardon or forgive, and forget and stay strong

I believe that relationship is the most crucial element to deal with first in becoming successful. The fact is that there are common issues in every relationship. Charity begins at home, and it will go a long way to solving problems in our work places, business environments, and in our society and nations.

As defined in dictionary.com, *relationship* is a connection, association, or involvement. It can be an emotional connection between individuals by blood or marriage. The British dictionary defines relationships as the state of being connected or related, or an association by blood or marriage. Merriam Webster's dictionary simply defines relationships as the way in which two or more people, groups, or countries interact with each other. Relationship may or may not include romantically or sexually.

The first relationships on earth are recorded in the first book of the Bible, Genesis. That is the relationship of God to man, and the relationship of husband and wife, the beginning of the family. In fact, the entire Bible paints a picture of God's tremendous love for His children in that He gave His only begotten Son, Jesus Christ, so that everyone might have a new relationship in the family of God by grace through faith. When we know Jesus, a good relationship with Him will sustain us through all other earthly relationships. A relationship with God is the only relationship that is guaranteed for all of eternity.

Companionship started with God after the creation of heaven and earth. God needed companionship with people, and said, "Let us make man in our own image." God instituted relationship, marriage, and family, but our adversary, the devil, and his servants, have their plans to destroy, kill, separate, and steal the joy of union. However, marriage and relationship are blessings and favour of God.

At every stage of life, our relationships and families present us with both joys and challenges. Learning to manage stress, to understand our own emotions and behaviours, and to communicate effectively can help strengthen our own emotional health, as well as our connections to the important people in our lives. It is my greatest desire to use my experience and wisdom to support and mentor our younger ones, to prepare their minds and their expectations before starting any relationship, and to support them in making wise decisions. It is my desire to teach them moral values to encourage them to stay out of trouble, to be successful in life and in their career, to stay employed and to become well distinguished entrepreneurs, while developing good character that will take them to the next level. It is to encourage and coach each person on how to relate effectively in any area of life, to love and be loved, to have patience, to be persistent and to persevere. Also, it is time to help other women like me who are facing challenges, for them to turn their situations to opportunities to learn and grow and be successful women and role models to younger ones. Everyone—young and old, ladies, gentlemen, and couples—can all attain greater levels of relationships with my *Imperfect Principles*.

This is not just for marriage relationships, but I believe everyone that is in any form of relationship can benefit from this book. This is an insight into various issues and questions to do with relationships. Having a relationship is to learn to develop. A place of marriage is a place of learning. There is no career or position in society that can stop or hinder any relationship unless we permit it. Over the years, Dwayne the Rock Johnson has been blessed with fame and wealth, but he says nothing matters more to him than his personal relationships.

I have confidence that these simple solutions in this book will prepare, build, maintain, and restore and refresh any relationship, for there is nothing too difficult for God to do, and all things are possible. I have practically seen broken homes and marriages restored, conflicts in workplaces resolved, and friendship regained by simple principles, words of wisdom, and prayers. I also discovered there are common issues for all relationships, such as lack of communication, misunderstanding, deception, bad influences, unforgiveness, bitterness, and so on. I believe these solutions will be a good tool to use to support and encourage others in relationships, in families (particularly young adults and couples), in the neighbourhood, in our communities, and within the society, and in bringing hope for today, tomorrow, and forever.

No matter how much we have achieved in any area of our lives, true fulfilment can only be found in the quality of our personal relationships with God and with others whom we have personal relationships with. Your past experiences don't have to limit your ability to create deeper, richer, and more fulfilling relationships. Yes, You CAN build and maintain healthy and better relationships. It is not easy, but it is POSSIBLE. Believe in yourself; life has taught me that you cannot control someone's loyalty. No matter how good you are to them, it does not mean that they will treat you the same. No matter how much they mean to you, it does not mean that they will value you the same. Situations and circumstances will make you stronger, even if it feels difficult, as it might just become a great opportunity for you to succeed in relationship.

"Always be yourself. Never try to hide who you are. The only shame is to have shame. Always stand up for what you believe in. Always question what other people tell you. Never regret the past; it's a waste of time. There's a reason for everything—every mistake, every moment of weakness, every terrible thing that has happened to you—so grow from it. The only way you can ever get the respect of others is when you show them that you respect yourself, and most importantly, do your thing and never apologise for being you."
– Unknown

Most of us are allured by the attractive notion that effortless relationships exist. Whether it be happily ever-after marriages, or friendships that last forever, or parent/child bonds, which supersede the need to understand each other, we'd all like to believe that our most intimate relationships are unconditional and strong enough to withstand whatever may come. However, at some point in our lives, most of us need to face the fact that relationships require effort to keep them strong and positive, and that even wonderful, strong relationships can be destroyed by neglect. When you are looking to improve a relationship, understanding your own personality type and the personality type of the other person involved in the relationship will bring a new dynamic to the situation, as this will allow better understanding and communication. Although the different types of relationships have very different characteristics and specific needs, there are two basic areas that seem to be critical in all relationships: expectations and communication. What do we expect from ourselves and the other person involved in the relationship? How do we communicate these expectations, and our feelings and opinions, to the person in the relationship? How does our personality type affect our expectations and methods of communication? Does our personality type affect whom we are romantically attracted to? How does it affect who our friends are, and whom we work with best?

Relationship is not only about marriage, as there are also different kinds of relationships: relationships in community/society, customer relationships, business relationships, working relationships, friend-ships, relationships with neighbours, relationships with parents, and relationship with God. The principles in the Bible, and wisdom for relationships that I have discovered, work similarly for everyone as we apply them to our lives, and I will be embarking on them section by section, so stay connected.

IMPERFECT PRINCIPLES

In life, no one is perfect—no individual, family, or any relationship of any kind is perfect. We are all different and from different backgrounds. We cannot change anybody, but we can change ourselves for the better. This is why I have chosen to use *IMPERFECT* Principles. There are challenges people face, in any relationship, that need solutions, and in my coaching and mentoring sessions, I help set goals and plan reasonable strategies for how to overcome anger, how to forgive and be free from bitterness, how to overcome fear, how to manage emotions, how to communicate, how to relate with spouse, children, friends, relations, and colleagues, how to love again, how to build trust, how you will be able to trust again, and how to keep safe in a relationship and not to suffer in silence.

Fifty-three years of my life experiences, and twenty-six years of marital life, has led me to have compassion for families, for single people, for married couples, for anyone wanting to build deeper relationships, and for families facing challenges in any area of their lives. I have special concern for women who are being limited in what they could do or become: women who have been told they cannot amount to anything; that they cannot succeed; that they cannot achieve. I would like to show that you can prove negative words and negative opinions of others wrong, and turn such negativity into positive. I have been there, stayed in it, and I have been able to overcome it by using other people's wisdom from their experiences to come up successful and stronger. I have used the 5Ds principles to overcome the negative experiences. I will also use these principles with my clients to develop their winning attitude. These 5D steps have been discussed in the earlier chapter, and are Dreams, Desire, Determination, Discipline, and Decision. These are steps I have taken personally that have helped me in my journey of life, especially during the times of negative experience, relationship and emotional trauma, and in my marital life. Yes, you can relate.

FACTS ABOUT MARRIED COUPLES

Husband and wife relationships are not as bad as others out there think. Marriage is a blessed and holy institution ordained by God. A faithful man and a virtuous woman will build their home with wisdom and the fear of God. The fear of God is the beginning of wisdom. The fear of God will make man to love his wife as himself. It is relationship with God and obeying His principles that really work best. Love one another; it is about patience, understanding, and endurance. It is about tolerance. It is not with provocation, arrogance, pride, competition, violence, pretence, deceit, or suffering in silence, but it is by prayers and seeking for help when needed. We all need one another. The male is for strength, provision, and protection, while the female is for comfort, nurturing, and support.

A wife is so precious to look for and to find, and that is why a husband is blessed and rewarded with favour. Before God can release such favour to man, he has to leave his dad and mum, and cleave to his wife, and he has to take full responsibility of a good thing, a diamond, a precious thing which he found. Favour comes with the wife a man finds, and that is the reason why a husband should love and cherish his wife, and a wife should respect and submit to her husband. A man finds a wife and obtains favour from God (Proverbs 18:22). If a man appreciates those two things, and treats his wife in a unique way, then the favour increases, and the favour expands and multiplies to another gift of God: children. Children are the gift of God that add no sorrow. Children are the heritage of God, and children are for signs and wonders. Children are the generational seeds. Children are the generational gifts from God.

In life, the race is not to the swift; the battle is not to the strong; the horse may be prepared for the day of battle, but victory is of the Lord (Ecclesiastes 9:11). It is only the home that the Lord builds that is built (Psalm 127:1). Except the Lord builds the house, they labour in vain that build it.

UNHEALTHY MARRIAGE RELATIONSHIPS

Some examples of unhealthy marriage relationships:

Independent – power couple. Both highly focused on careers or separate social lives, and meet when it's convenient for both, and love is not priority.

Co-dependent – cannot function without the other person. Each feels anxiety or depression when they are not around each other.

Dominating – someone who controls and sets rules for the relationship, and the partner follows.

Rebound – just gone through a breakup and need love to cover up the pain. This is built on the fear of facing the reality of a recent breakup, and does not consider whether the new person is right for them or not.

Open – no commitment; working hard but nothing to show for it; toxic relationship though attractive to one another; have drastically different morals, integrity, and opinions such that all they do is fight. They bring out the worst in each other and can't stay away from each other. These leave each person emotionally, mentally, and physically immobile or traumatised. A relationship that is a temporary good distraction for a while, and it's fun for now, but there is no plan for the future.

Basically friends – but no intimacy and not sexually oriented; blood runs cold; purely sex but not compelled to explore each other's chemistry in all areas.

Prize possession – when looking for rich people or very good-looking persons; good on paper to impress or influence others but not connected to one another.

Relationship is very crucial to success in life. It is relationship skills that everyone needs to implement to gain friendship, love, partnership, and colleagues at work. In this book, I will also share with you the issues that affect any relationship and how to overcome them. If there is good relationship at home, there will be a good relationship at work, in the community, and within the society and nation. Charity begins at home.

> *"Let us take time to get acquainted with our families. We are not machines. We are not robots. The secret of a happy home is that members of the family learn to give and receive love. Let us take time to express our love in a thousand ways."*
> – Billy Graham

SWOT ANALYSIS OF A RELATIONSHIP

The *strengths, weaknesses, opportunities, and treats* in a relationship. A personal SWOT analysis is a great tool for evaluating yourself and your life in general, or for a specific aspect that you may want to change. It helps you think things through, get a more balanced perspective, and then consider what to do in a relationship. You may be familiar with the use of SWOT analysis in business, yet you can apply it to your personal life too. The thinking behind the SWOT analysis is what counts, not the content. It allows you to take a more balanced view of the situation in relationships.

Strengths – For a personal SWOT analysis, the strengths are everything good about you. For example, for a job change, you can list specific skills, experience, flexibility in location, willingness to re-train, and so on. If the analysis is about a personal situation, such as your relationship with someone, you would list the good points pertinent to the relationship: the good times you've had together, shared interests, how you help each other.

Weaknesses – Weaknesses are where the problems lie, either with you, or the situation. The job change scenario may highlight your need to stay near an aging parent, or a lack of a required qualification. A SWOT analysis on a relationship may list poor communication as a weakness.

Opportunities – Opportunities are things that haven't happened; you may or may not have noticed them. This is your chance to identify and think them through. Who do you know that could help you get a new job? What courses are available? Would counselling help your relationship improve, or perhaps just making more time for each other?

Threats – Threats are also things that haven't happened but could hamper the success of what you want to do. When considering a job change, you might hate the new company or role, or the job may not last. For your relationship, threats are the chance you may grow apart, or your partner may meet someone else.

Relationships are a very meaningful part of our lives and can bring us a great deal of happiness and fulfilment. Strong connections with our loved ones, friends, and work colleagues allow us to be at our healthiest and most productive. For many, these relationships offer an important source of advice, guidance, love, and support. However, fulfilling and supportive relationships don't come automatically, and they require good social skills and a great deal of time and energy to stay strong and go the distance. Sometimes, meaningful connections break down, which can leave people feeling lonely, disappointed, and unsure of what to do.

In some cases, our relationships may not be fulfilling our expectations, which can impact our happiness and life satisfaction. On the other hand, some people may crave close friendships and/or romantic relationships but find them very difficult to come by. Whatever the relationship issue, there is help available in the form of relationship counselling. In this setting, a counsellor will work with couples or individuals to explore their needs and what they want from their relationships, while offering support and advice to help them get their relationship(s) back on track.

From the second we were born, we crave relationships. We need to feel connected to other people. We need to feel love and acceptance. Naturally, the first relationships we have are with our parents. We look to them for care, and they nurture us. We learn so much from them—good and bad—depending upon their beliefs and morals. As we grow older, we develop friendships— both platonic and romantic.

Many of us become parents ourselves. We continue to learn from every person we develop a relationship with. And then there are acquaintances—people we know. We might hang out with them sometimes, but their lives don't really intertwine with ours. They're usually not our first choice to go to dinner with. Their life struggles don't personally affect us in any way.

We learn to share. We learn teamwork. We develop likes and dislikes. We tend to gravitate towards people we look up to. This could also be people we fear. I always told my kids, "Be careful of who you hang out with, because you will develop some of their traits." It's just human nature. I think that's one of the reasons why it's so easy for couples to finish each other's sentences. The more time you spend with someone, the more like them you become. I believe that the relationships we have with others determine our true character. Family and friends will be there in our times of struggle; strangers and acquaintances will scarcely be seen. In the movie, *It's a Wonderful Life*, Clarence, the angel, writes, "Remember, George, no man is a failure who has friends." With friends and people by our sides, we can accomplish anything.

It's important that we build strong relationships with those we love. They are the ones that matter the most to us. We should always treat them as such. Never take them for granted. Value the unique aspect of each individual. Can you imagine how boring life would be if we were all the same? Treat everybody with respect. Accept people where they are. Allow them to make their own choices in life. Remember, you can't change anyone but yourself, so concentrate on being the best person and the best friend you can be—and you'll have no problem establishing and retaining real, long-lasting relationships. Most of us want to find a partner to share our lives with. When we finally fall in love and commit to a relationship that we believe will last us to old age, we have expectations that we will act together to realise our dreams. Inevitably though, every couple will experience relationship difficulties. Couples will always be confronted and sometimes overwhelmed by challenges they face. Mostly, they are able to deal with them and move on. However, sometimes these challenges leave each partner feeling alienated and alone, and unable to sort out the issues no matter how hard they try. The same old arguments occur, with the same frustrating outcomes, and both partners can feel stuck. As time goes on, one or both may start considering separation. Sadly, separation and divorce statistics are high, yet many of the difficulties that threaten the survival of relationships can be sorted out, with the right help.

YOU CAN COMMUNICATE EFFECTIVELY

> "Let the words of my mouth, and the meditation of my heart, be acceptable in thy sight, O Lord, my strength, and my redeemer."
> Psalms 19:14 KJV

Communication is the most crucial element in building and maintaining relationships. Remember that the goal of effective communication should be mutual understanding and finding a solution that pleases both parties—not *winning* the argument or *being right.*

Rapport Skills

What we say can create or destroy rapport, but interestingly, only 7% of communication is the spoken words. Our body language and our tone of voice are more important than the actual words spoken. Have you ever noticed how conversation just seems to flow when two people are in rapport? Their bodies, as well as their words, match each other. Just watch a couple in a restaurant, or friends meeting in a pub; they dance the dance of rapport! Picking up their glasses in unison, matching each other's body language and speaking styles—it's all part of the dance!

So, what is rapport? It is *"the process of establishing and maintaining a relationship of mutual trust and understanding between two or more people; the ability to generate responses from another person." Introducing NLP,* by Joseph O'Connor & John Seymour.

The ability to communicate non-verbally is also an important skill to learn and enhance. This type of communication is more powerful than mere words. Emotions and messages are conveyed through our body language, so this skill is highly visual. Communicate properly through appropriate use of facial expressions, gestures, eye contact, body movements, and our voice. Communication supports transparency.

Many of us have been taught that if you want to succeed as a sales professional, all you need to do is be friendly, polite, and knowledgeably explain the benefits of your products and services to potential clients. You might need to wine and dine them, understand what their interests are, and if they have a partner, a family, etc. Is that what rapport is? No, it isn't. Having an understanding of a client's interests won't do you any harm, but rapport is a much deeper communication skill. Living things do not communicate with language alone. Think about animals and plants that don't have a language; they still communicate with other members of their species and with others outside their species. They do this through non-verbal behaviour, such as changing colour. Humans communicate non-verbally too!

Have you ever admired someone who just knows when to ask the *killer question*, or when to stay silent, or when to stop pushing their client? It's all about reading someone's non-verbal communications. By heightening your sensory perception (your awareness of the senses such as seeing, hearing, and feeling), you will develop the skills you admire and be able to develop great relationships. Rapport skills enable you to quickly put others at ease and create trust. These skills allow you to get on with anyone anywhere, and greatly increase your confidence and effectiveness. It also makes it easier for others to communicate with you. Mastering the skill of rapport building requires sensory perception and behaviour flexibility on your part.

The building blocks for matching are body language, posture, weight distribution, gestures, arms and hands, legs and feet, facial expressions, eye contact, and breathing rate, as well as voice quality, volume, tone, pitch, and tempo. Leading enhances rapport by changing the other person's behaviour, by getting them to follow your lead (e.g. leading them from slumping, into a more upright posture, or leading them from speaking quietly to speaking more loudly). Having rapport and being able to lead others makes it easier to achieve mutually desired outcomes, such as reaching agreement. If you are prepared to use these skills consciously, you can create rapport with whoever you choose. You don't have to like the person to create rapport; you are simply building a bridge to understand them better. You will not know that it is effective or what results you'll get unless you try it! The dance of rapport is what we do naturally. It allows you to join the other person in their model of the world. Rapport needs your flexibility of thought and behaviour. Notice what happens when people get on well—they tend to match. Notice the opposite when people are in disagreement—they mismatch. Notice when you are not getting on with someone and try matching! Make it easy for others to communicate with you by practicing rapport. Liking the other person is not a prerequisite for rapport.

For example, if you're having a conflict in a romantic relationship, it helps to hold hands or stay physically connected as you talk. This can remind you that you still care about each other and generally support each other. Keep in mind that it's important to remain respectful of the other person, even if you don't like their actions.

Telling the truth in a sensible way about how we feel can benefit a relationship—don't be afraid to say the truth to one another, for the truth will build trust and understanding in relationship. It demands understanding and patience; keep sharing, keep talking, keep listening, keep reasoning, and peace that passes understanding will garrison your heart.

Creating and honouring time for one another will give opportunity to understand your differences and appreciate them. There is a saying that the way to a man's heart is through his stomach, but the way to a woman's heart is through her ears—a sacred space, where you set aside time each week to sit without distraction and talk about your relationship. A relationship needs attention, and the level of the attention to one another determines the closeness and understanding in that relationship.

Giving respect and consideration is important in a relationship. When partners hold each other as their priority, respect is a natural eventuality. True love is about putting someone else's needs before your own. Give support rather than undermining the other. Be considerate and respect their needs, giving time to grow or heal instead of condemning, judging, gossiping, or saying negative words to one another. Humour brings a lot less tension and a lot more forward motion. Finding the opportunity inside the obstacle is a lesson that carries great weight over time. Nagging and complaining doesn't work; only prayer works. If you prayed more, you'd have a lot less to grumble, complain, nag, and nit-pick about. It's your decision.

Positive praying is more effective than positive thinking. All the positive thinking in the world is not enough to change your husband or your wife—or your child or your friend or your situation— and moreover, you cannot change them. Positive thinking can change you, but it won't change somebody else. What we are saying to one another matters. Words are very powerful. Words are sharp. Words can kill or give life. Words can destroy or build. Words can lift or pull someone down. Words can damage a relationship, so watch what you say to one another.

How Can I Improve My Communication with My Spouse?

At the start of the relationship, conversations are exciting and fun. Both of you spend a lot of time getting to know each other. But as time goes by, lovers forget to ask the same questions again. We're all changing all the time, in our preferences and the way we look at life. Don't assume you know everything about each other or your romance will start to stagnate. You must do all you can to stay connected so that one of you does not start to confide in some other person who seems more understanding.

How Do I Prevent Arguments with My Spouse?

Settling scores is a guaranteed way to cause relationship issues or marital problems. Power battles and/or scoring points for whatever reason, treating your partner with contempt, wanting to be right all of the time, wanting to win an argument, manipulating your partner or situations to get your own way, undermining the other person that you are supposed to love, all create problems within a marriage. Avoid using your partner or spouse deliberately to get what you want. Avoid controlling your partner or spouse, and avoid all forms of abuse, whether financial, physical, mental and/or emotional.

What Are the Better Ways to Discuss with My Spouse Without Arguments?

Know what you want to achieve in the ideal circumstances, and consider alternative solutions or outcomes that you can live with. Know what you're willing to give up, and remember: it's not about *winning*. Consider how you could be biased, and avoid this. Work out what you want to say beforehand, and write it down if necessary. Consider your tone of voice—as discussed earlier, how you say things is really important. Practise responding calmly to any potentially adverse reactions (REALLY important!). Be prepared to learn from any criticism—accept it, or simply cast it aside if it is destructive, and make sure you're sober. Don't have a difficult conversation when you've had a drink.

Invite your partner to help you to both get the best out of the *chat*. Give your partner plenty of time to express him or herself, and avoid interrupting at all costs! Interrupting your partner is sure to lead to an argument; listen for underlying emotional needs that haven't been met. When you've been married or in a relationship for some time, it's all too easy to lose sight of the fact that you both need to have your essential emotional needs met in balance. Ask questions in a neutral tone of voice, and avoid making assumptions. Remember: listening does not imply that you're agreeing! Repeat what you think you've heard, in your own words, and summarise to check that you have understood as much as possible. Ask how the other's solution will solve the problem, without arguments. Ask and ensure that the person allows you to do the same—offer solutions that will prevent you arguing as a couple.

How Can Parents Communicate with Their Children?

Parents should appreciate the uniqueness of each child. Every child needs to feel secure. Parents need to provide that feeling of security at all times. Children need their parents to listen to them. Listening is a crucial aspect of understanding and nurturing a child. Your child has his/her own uniqueness and personality, so take time to learn and understand them. What makes him/her tick? What makes him/her sad? What is his/her dream? There is a lot of pressure these days on children. There's pressure from school; there's peer pressure, societal pressure, television, social media, etc. An adjustment required is for the parent to do less talking and listen more. Children need their parents to look out for them, to listen in a supportive way and to be there to offer comfort.

Make no assumption that what beliefs you hold dear have automatically been transferred to your children, as this is not always the case. Be open minded to the fact that your older child may have a different point of view on some aspects of life, and that they will express this as they grow older and begin to analyse what you have been teaching and modelling to them. However, eventually, and in most cases, they will usually come back to hold dear what you have taught them as important. Avoid using a bully pulpit of do as I say, not as I do, which is very ineffective and could be damaging.

Comparing our kids or our style of parenting with others could be self-defeating, as it encourages unhealthy competition. We should learn from others but don't compare, and we should not play favouritism among our children. Children want your acknowledgment and approval. Never be ashamed to hug your kids and say you love them; never play favouritism with your children, and don't compare your children with others. Love them the way they are, and find a unique way to correct them when correction is needed.

Do not be harsh with your child. Manage your tone of voice when correcting or communicating with your child. Sometimes our words might be appropriate, but our tone may not be. Harsh words stir up anger, but a gentle answer turns away wrath.

Love and respect your spouse. Your children learn quickly how to do the same from you. If they are raised within a loving marriage, they have a great model for their own future relationship.

How Can I Inspire Manners in My Children?

1. When you come back home to your children from an outing, greet your children or even hug them. This should help develop their sense of love and self-worth.

2. Be good to your neighbours and never backbite. Never speak ill of other drivers when on the road. Your children would listen, absorb, and emulate.

3. When calling your parents, encourage your children to speak to them. When visiting your parents, take your children with you. The more they see you take care of your parents, the more they will learn to take care of you.

4. When driving them to school, don't always play albums or CDs in the car. Rather, tell them some motivational stories yourself. This

will have a greater impact.

5. Read to them a short story and even a scripture a day—it doesn't take much time, but it is very impactful in creating strong bonds and wonderful memories.

6. Comb your hair, clean your teeth, and wear presentable clothes, even if sitting at home and not going out for the day. They need to learn that being clean and tidy has nothing to do with going out!

7. Try not to blame or comment on every word or action they say or do. Learn to overlook and let go sometimes. This certainly builds their self-confidence.

8. Ask your children's permission before entering their rooms. Don't just knock and enter, but wait for a verbal permission. They will learn to do the same when wanting to enter your room.

9. Apologise to your children if you made a mistake. This teaches them to be humble and to be polite.

10. Don't be sarcastic or make fun of their views or feelings, even if you "didn't mean it" and was "only joking." It really hurts.

11. Show respect for your children's privacy. It's important for their sense of value and self-esteem.

12. Don't expect that they will listen or understand the first time. Don't take it personal. But be patient and consistent.

13. Pray with them. Show them how to pray. Lead by example.

14. Ask your children to discuss their daily plans after morning prayers. Children without concrete daily plans usually join others

in executing theirs. They fall easy to peer pressure.

15. Hold them and bless them, especially every morning.

NEXT CHAPTER

People hide from their emotions and allow those emotions to govern their lives uncontrollably, leading to many unresolved conflicts, inner conflicts, and conflicts with others. As a result of this, the person who is in touch with their emotions, who knows how to control and understand them, and who is able to detach themselves from their feelings, is often viewed as stable, professional, and reliable, in business or in private life. And they really are, because they don't allow emotions to rule their lives. In the next chapter, we will work together as we learn to manage our emotions.

CHAPTER 7

YES, YOU CAN MANAGE YOUR EMOTIONS, AND BECOME A BETTER PERSON

Emotional responsibility is the most important ingredient for creating a healthy relationship. When people do not take responsibility for their own feelings, they tend to try and make others responsible for their own happiness. As adults, happiness, emotional safety, and self-esteem also come from how we treat ourselves and others. Therefore, we should not be abandoning ourselves but, rather, we should love and value ourselves.

EMOTIONAL INTELLIGENCE

 People have got used to hiding from their emotions or letting their emotions govern their lives. This leads to many unresolved conflicts, inner and with others. As a result, the person who is in touch with their emotions, who knows how to control and understand them, and who is able to detach themselves from their feelings, is often viewed as stable, professional, and reliable. They do not allow emotions to rule their lives. This doesn't mean that these people don't feel anything—it's just that they know how to properly handle their emotions and use them in the most constructive way. Becoming familiar with your emotions also enables you to understand why others sometimes behave the way they do, so you can use this knowledge to deepen your personal and professional relationships, and to make real connections with people around you. Emotional intelligence isn't something people are born with—it's a learned skill, and if you want, you can adopt it too!

According to **Margaret Paul, Ph.D., relationship expert, best-selling author, and co-creator of the powerful Inner Bonding® self-healing process**, relationship problems are a by-product of emotional problems and emotional self-abandonment. Emotional self-abandonment generally occurs in four ways: ignoring your feelings by staying in your head rather than being present in your body; judging yourself; turning to various addictions to avoid your feelings; and making others responsible for your feelings. However, by doing your own inner work to become an emotionally responsible, kind and loving person with yourself and with each other, you can create a healthy, loving relationship! So therefore, start learning how to love and connect with yourself so that you can connect with others.

Emotional intelligence at work and in business is to understand the feelings of communication between boss and staff. It is the ability and awareness to read non-verbal cues (body language); the ability to handle and control annoyance, joy, anger, frustration, and other emotions; recognising and reacting to words and actions in the workplace. It is the ability to manage, use, identify and understand emotions, have compassion, resolve conflict or misunderstanding, and relieve stress. Intellectual intelligence is not the only criteria for being successful in life; there is also emotional intelligence.

5 IMPORTANT SKILLS FOR EMOTIONAL INTELLIGENCE

The ability to show emotional intelligence requires five important skills that every individual should apply in building and keeping healthy relationships.

The first skill is the ability to manage stress. The second skill is the ability to recognise and manage our emotions. Emotional awareness helps us understand our needs and motivations apart from having good communication skills. Understanding yourself means assessing your emotions and feelings and turning them to positive ones. Seek encouragement and motivate yourself, thereby reducing stress. Find what is energizing or soothing that appeals to your senses of touch, taste, sound, and smell. For example, if you respond more to sound, then listen to music. The third important skill is the ability to communicate non-verbally. This type of communication is more powerful than mere words. What you say might convey something different depending on how you say it. Use non-verbal communication to gain attention, connect, and build trust. Emotions and messages are conveyed through our body language, so this skill is highly visual. Communicate properly through appropriate use of facial expressions, gestures, eye contact, body movements, and tone of voice. The fourth skill is the ability to use humour and play in the relationship. Good humour lifts up a distressing situation in a relationship and gives us a feeling of relief from a challenging experience. Individuals are able to iron out some differences through humour and playfulness, taking relationship problems lightly. The last skill is the ability to resolve conflicts in the relationship.

Our affiliations with people in personal and professional aspects do not always run smoothly. Demonstrate emotional intelligence during conflicts by properly responding to and facing any dispute or disagreements with others. Understand the fact that conflicts are inevitable but manageable. And when proper emotional intelligence is applied in dealing with it, conflicts would turn out to be productive and helpful in strengthening work relationships. Manifesting proper emotional intelligence in building relationships brings about many advantageous results for the individuals and the connection they are creating. Professional relationships are strengthened because there is understanding and open communication among co-workers. This makes it easy for team members to iron out any glitches at work and even mend wounded feelings. Good and healthy work relationships create a blissful and healthy work environment, where individuals are more comfortable working with each other.

EFFECTS OF UNMANAGED EMOTIONS

Unmanaged emotions lead to unmanaged stress, depression, anxiety, and a feeling of isolation. It also affects physical wellbeing, causes health problems, speeds up the aging process, contributes to high blood pressure, suppresses the immune system, and increases the risk of stroke or heart attack.

HOW CAN I RESOLVE CONFLICT?

Forgive, focus on the present, and reason about the matter. Arguments take energy and time, and are not worth your time and energy. Tackle the unresolved conflicts, using humour. Using humour the right way lessens the burden of the conflict, lessens your worries, strengthens your mood, reduces anxiety or stress, keeps the nervous system balanced, develops your creativity, and relaxes everyone involved. Laughter helps you survive the major setback. Involve yourself in activities you enjoy. Have fun, and hang out with fun-loving people.

STRESS MANAGEMENT IN RELATIONSHIP

Poor stress management is a foundational cause of many anger problems, and individuals who have experienced trauma often have multiple layers of chronic stress in their daily lives. The primary stress of the traumatic situation itself can be psychologically overwhelming and debilitating for some time. This causes one to be at a psychological disadvantage when encountering new challenges that come with everyday, non-traumatic life. Additionally, the stressors of everyday life fluctuate and add, from time to time, their own overwhelming effects that may peak and push the limits of one's abilities to cope. Stress, whether from inside or outside your relationship, is likely to affect the way you think, feel, and behave. This invariably impacts on your partner and your relationship, creating a vicious circle. Relationship stress can be caused by a drip-drip effect of, for example, never-ending criticism, feeling unheard, disagreements over chores, sexual problems, work-related problems, financial difficulties, arguments, etc. It can also come about as a result of a crisis, such as an affair, sudden illness, the death of a loved one, or other family problems. Avoiding issues can provide temporary relief, but this may lead, in the long term, to a build-up of stress and reduced resilience when confronted with stressful situations. There are also physical consequences because the impact of such stress can make a person ill.

Other factors that induce or increase stress include environmental pollutants, such as noise. Some people are naturally more sensitive to noise than others, but there is a limit to what's healthy. Dehydration is also a factor. Your body consists of about 60% water if you're a man, and 70% if you're a woman, so of course, it's going to be stressed if it's dehydrated. Lack of sufficient sleep, vigorous and excessive exercise, poor diet or poor quality food that is not fresh, that is full of antibiotics and/or pesticides, food intolerance or allergies, mal absorption (nutrients are poorly absorbed), mal digestion (poor digestion), other allergies, and also exposure to extreme temperatures, or damp and other poor housing conditions, disruption of the *natural* light cycle (for example, shift work), addictions, inflammation (swelling, sensitivity, pain, heat in your body) are all inducers of stress.

WHAT CAN I DO TO EFFECTIVELY DEAL WITH RELATIONSHIP STRESS?

Calm yourself or do whatever you can to calm your partner—as human beings, we're much better at finding solutions when we're calm. Accept that your partner cannot read your mind. There is now evidence that *reading someone's face* can be unreliable. Understand that your partner is going to react. Therefore, deal with stress and solve problems differently than you would, even if you don't like or understand their ways! Realise that your and your partner's time scale may be very different. Write down your thoughts—it will help you to be more objective. Address any external sources of stress, state clearly if something is really unacceptable to you, and do take care of yourself. This means getting enough sleep, eating well, and exercising regularly. Engage in meaningful and enjoyable activities, even if it seems too much of an effort to start with, and consider taking some gentle, natural remedies.

You can improve your emotions by writing your feelings and thoughts; giving yourself a break; being aware of your present feelings, both conscious and unconscious; listening to your body sensations (it allows you to process your reasoning power); connecting your feelings to your thoughts; not being judgmental of your feelings; and finding ways to encourage yourself.

HELPING YOUR CHILDREN WITH THEIR EMOTIONS

In addition to communicating effectively with your child, and thereby enhancing their emotional well-being as discussed in the previous chapter, acknowledge your child's emotions. According to Dr. Laura Markham, of high parenting advice, support is the most important aspect of nurturing emotions in children.

Teach your children how to solve problems, and how to tolerate their emotions without the use of aggressive or harmful actions.

All of us have experienced moments of emotional pain. We need to understand that it is not our fault, and that we can overcome emotional pain. Our emotions can get better so that we can be free to relate with others effectively, to understand others and to become better.

SOME OF THE WAYS TO OVERCOME OUR EMOTIONS ARE BY AFFIRMATIONS, PRAYERS AND MEDITATIONS

Affirmations penetrate deep into your subconscious, passively, without you taking conscious action, and imprint within it a new set of thinking patterns—a new set of thinking patterns that will allow you to get in touch with your emotions, become better aware of how they impact your behaviour, and enable you develop healthier means of handling your emotions. These affirmations will activate the parts of your mind responsible for the way you're dealing with your emotions. You will develop a clear understanding of why you feel the way you feel, and the mechanisms activated when an emotion gets too *loud*. You will be able to choose healthier ways of dealing with it and be better able to understand others. This will bring about significant improvement in your relationships. You will no longer be controlled by someone's emotional reaction because, by learning to recognise your own emotions and reactions, you will be better equipped to understand others. By not letting the emotions govern your life, you will understand what *having peace of mind* means. You will no longer be finding yourself overwhelmed by sadness, stress, or anger—you will learn to neutrally observe them and to let them go without them leaving a significant mark on you.

AFFIRMATION 11

I am aware of my emotions. I am alert to the feelings of those around me. I pick up on mood changes in myself and in others. I can reason with my emotions. My emotions are under control. I manage my feelings. Understanding emotions comes easily to me. I regulate the emotions of my peers. I respond appropriately to my emotions. I accurately interpret the emotions of others. I will focus more on my feelings. I will acknowledge my emotions. I will react to the emotions of those around me. I am becoming confident in my emotional perception. I will intelligently evaluate others' sentiments. I will be seen as emotionally aware. My emotions will be manageable. My ability to get along with others will improve.

I will assess the emotions of my peers. I will be able to build stronger relationships with others. I am naturally attentive to emotions. Emotional intelligence comes second-nature to me. I am tuned-in to the feelings of others. I simply manage my emotions. I just naturally know my emotional boundaries. I instinctively read my peers' emotions. Others see me as emotionally aware. I am tuned-in to my emotional well-being. I have full confidence in my emotional judgment, for emotions are easy to dissect.

A REAL WOMAN, A VIRTUOUS WIFE AND A ROLE MODEL

A real woman is always there; she represents a strong link in the chain that holds those close to her together. She embraces the many roles she plays and is actively present, whether as a wife, mother, daughter, sister, girlfriend, or friend.

Permit me to share this little story with you. Once upon a time, a man went with his wife in their car to a fuel station. While they were buying the fuel, the man discovered that it was his wife's ex-boyfriend that was attending to them. He then smiled and turned to his wife and said, "You would have ended up marrying that petrol attendant," but the wife smiled and said, "If I had married him, he would be the one sitting by the steering of this car." This woman understands the power of a woman—she gets it! She knows who she is, and she knows that a genuine and real woman has in her the capacity to produce much out of little.

I do not underestimate my power as a woman. I will not be reduced to nothing or think I'm worthless by meaningless singers out there that think I am men's problem or equivalent to money or sex. There is more to me than meets the eye. Come with me in this chapter, where I share with you the quality of a woman. Women are unique, beautiful, and precious. Women were empowered by God to do many things; they are creative, industrious, caring and loving, according to Proverbs 31. Women are beautiful on the inside and outside, so ladies need to be constantly reminded of this by their parents first. Every female is peculiar, and each is a role model; they just need to appreciate that. Good character brings out a good woman and lady. They have moral values that they need to develop and appreciate. This will take time to develop, and it takes patience and endurance. Character can be developed, so in this chapter, I share the stories of some of the real women in the Bible.

A real woman, to me, is described in Proverbs 31, verses10–31, as follows: Verse 10(b) A wife of noble character, who can find? She is worth far more than rubies. 11 Her husband has full confidence in her and lacks nothing of value. 12 She brings him good, not harm, all the days of her life. 13 She selects wool and works with eager hands. 14 She is like the merchant ships, bringing her food from afar. 15 She gets up while it is still night; she provides food for her family and portions for her female servants. 16 She considers a field and buys it; out of her earnings she plants a vineyard. 17 She sets about her work vigorously; her arms are strong for her tasks. 18 She sees that her trading is profitable, and her lamp does not go out at night. 19 In her hand she holds the distaff and grasps the spindle with her fingers. 20 She opens her arms to the poor and extends her hands to the needy. 21 When it snows, she has no fear for her household, for all of them are clothed in scarlet. 22 She makes coverings for her bed; she is clothed in fine linen and purple. 23 Her husband is respected at the city gate; he takes his seat among the elders of the land. 24 She makes linen garments and sells them and supplies the merchants with sashes. 25 She is clothed with strength and dignity; she can laugh at the days to come. 26 She speaks with wisdom, and faithful instruction is on her tongue. 27 She watches over the affairs of her household and does not eat the bread of idleness. 28 Her children arise and call her blessed; her husband also, and he praises her: 29 "Many women do noble things, but you surpass them all." 30 Charm is deceptive, and beauty is fleeting; but a woman who fears the Lord is to be praised. 31 Honour her for all that her hands have done, and let her works bring her praise at the city gate.

A real woman has a defined purpose, whether personally or professionally. She has great goals and desires. She knows that with the right amount of inspiration and motivation, anything is possible, and is willing to do what it takes to make her dreams a reality. A real woman is strong and independent; she is determined, driven, and able to accomplish great feats. She's very good at taking care of herself and doing her own thing. A real woman has patience, for herself and for those around her, and she knows how to play it cool. In the face of adversity, she is able to tap the proper resources to conquer any problem, instead of just giving up.

A real woman values a real man; she appreciates and respects the value and worth of the man in her life. She knows that part of being a great woman is recognising and embracing the qualities of a great man. She does not need a man in her life to be happy, but if she has one, she stands by him. She believes in his purpose and who he is, which makes going in the same direction with him that much easier. She's going to build her man up and support him in such a way that motivates him to want to be the type of man worthy of standing beside someone like her.

A real woman loves deeply. She is honest and upfront. She recognises the destructiveness behind undisclosed expectations. She's straightforward and respectful about setting boundaries and the tempo of her relationships early on. She's the type of woman you won't catch in a lie. When you're honest, you don't have to remember what you said or cover your tracks at all. A real woman has a healthy handle on her emotions. She does away with toxic relationships. She knows how to weather the storm correctly. If there are any shortfalls on the emotional front, she recognises them and adjusts accordingly. She has strong will; she fights for the things she truly believes in, and stands by the people she cares about. Practicing the art of gratitude, she knows it's important to show people they matter. She says the words, *thank you*, a lot.

She doesn't need anyone's approval when it comes to the choices she makes; she thinks deeply about things, meditating. She finds that *alone time* to gather her thoughts. She's the type of person who is very careful about her words and actions, and thinks about the cause and effect of them. She's well read, educating herself and upgrading her understanding and knowledge. She's smart, and not just book smart, but she accepts the fact she doesn't know everything, and makes an effort to learn. She's constantly trying to improve and better herself and learn as much as she can.

She forgives herself and others. She's not perfect. She'll be the first to apologise when she's wrong. She also will forgive you when you make a mistake. She has healthy relationships. She knows that who you are friends with will influence where you go. She isn't negative, nor does she gossip.

She looks great but knows and demonstrates that inner beauty is supreme. One of the main characteristics of a real woman is her ability to give inner beauty importance over outer beauty, because it's the inner beauty that always lasts, and not how *hot* your body is, or how *great* your fashion sense is. This is the kind of woman a real man sees but won't imagine sex instantly.

Be an Esther and be bold and courageous enough to stand for the truth, to voice your opinion and fight for the good of others. If God has put you in a position, it is for a purpose. Be a Ruth and be loyal in all your relationships; walk the extra mile and don't quit when things get tough; someday, you'll see why it was all worth the effort. Be a Lydia and be hospitable; let your hands be generous; let your hearts be big enough to help anyone in need. Joy is greatest when shared. Be a Hannah and never cease to pray. It will never be in vain. Be a

Mary, humble and submissive. You don't have to be great for God to use you and make you great. You just need to obey. Be a Dorcas and use your talents, however small it may seem, to bring a smile on someone's face. You'll never know how much it can mean to someone. Be an Abigail and remember how the right decision can turn your life around for good. Be wise like Elizabeth, and never doubt what God can do. Miracles do happen. Allow God, like Mary Magdalene, and never let your mistakes or other people's opinions stop you from experiencing true joy in Jesus Christ. Be a Rebecca and never forget that true beauty lies within.

EXCEPTIONAL MAN, HUSBAND AND FATHER

God came up with the idea of male leadership. He created Adam first before he created Eve, and made Adam to be physically stronger than Eve. This does not diminish a woman's strength or purpose in any way, and an exceptional man knows this. An exceptional man knows that both male and female are to submit to one another in Christ Jesus, and are both co-heirs of the grace of God.

Exceptional Man

God has a purpose in male leadership in our society, in families, and in raising men and future generations of male leaders. All through Bible scripture, we have seen patriarchs, prophets, kings, priests, judges, Jesus' disciples, and other leaders who made significant impact within the society. An exceptional man is a positive role model to young men. A God lover: a man who fears God and prioritises his relationship with God above others because he realises that his strength, gentleness, wisdom, courage, and abilities come from God.

Exceptional Husband

An exceptional husband is one who loves God so much that it shows in the way he loves and prioritises his wife and family and stays faithful to his wife. He makes time for his wife and spends quality time with her. He is a good communicator, listening carefully to his wife and to her concerns. He is very much interested in what concerns his wife. She will be able to share her precious thoughts and feelings with him. The Bible makes it clear in Ephesians 5:22–6:4 that the husband is the head of his family, the leader of his household. It says in verse 23–25 that the husband is the head of the wife, as Christ is the head of the Church, and that the husband should love his wife as Christ loves the Church.

According to the great Victorian preacher, C.H. Spurgeon: *"A husband loves his wife with a constant love...He will not cast her away tomorrow having loved her today. He does not vary in his affection. He may change in his display of affection, but the affection itself is still the same. A husband loves his wife with an enduring love; it never will die out. He says, 'Till death us do part will I cherish thee'.... A husband loves his wife with a hearty love, with a love that is true and intense. It is not mere lip service. He does not merely speak, but he acts; he is ready to provide for her wants; he will defend her character; he will vindicate her honour; because his heart is set upon her. It is not merely with the eye that he delights now and then to glance upon her, but his soul has her continually in his remembrance—she has a mansion in his heart from which she can never be cast away. She has become a portion of himself; she is a member of his body, she is a part of his flesh and of his bones."*

Exceptional Father

An exceptional father does not take his role and leadership of his family lightly. In his book, *Being a Dad Who Leads*, John MacArthur says, *"No duty in life is most important or sacred than my role as a husband and father."*

According to the Bible, a father's ultimate leadership in the home begins by loving his wife, the mother of his children. Even where his wife is not the biological mother of all his children in the household, a father has ultimate responsibility to model Christ's love to his family by loving his wife tenderly and by loving his children. The presence of the father's spiritual and pastoral leadership in the home will affect the character of his children and the adults they become.

"The essence of parental love is recognizing that
we are the dispensers of God's grace into our children's lives.
They learn to identify and reverence God's character
through the way we treat them..."
– Brian Chapell

Ephesians 6:4 admonishes fathers:

"Fathers, do not provoke your children to anger, but bring them up in the discipline and instruction of the Lord."

So, an exceptional father sees to his children's spiritual, physical, emotional, and self-esteem needs and overall wellbeing by being involved, and modelling love, gentleness, acceptance, care, tenderness, integrity, godly character, godly discipline, courage, and Christlikeness, helping his children to love and trust God.

The children blossom when their father acknowledges and appreciates them. It helps the children to build their confidence, and it motivates them not to give up in doing the right thing.

"An exceptional father encourages and builds his children up rather than discouraging them." Colossians 3:21.

"He is involved with everything about his children, including their education." Deut. 6:6–7. For example, if your child has a talent and they love a certain hobby, give attention to it and help them to excel. Carve out regular quality time for your family, having a strong bond with family; embrace other family ties such as grandparents, aunties, uncles, cousins, and in-laws. An exceptional father gives his children guidance and direction, setting appropriate boundaries as they grow up. Children need to make decisions, such as choosing friends, social groups, and social activities, and they need to do this carefully and with parental guidance and supervision.

"An exceptional father puts God first and treats his children as gifts." Deuteronomy 6:5–6. He relies on strength from God to fulfil his role as father adequately. Therefore, he realises that his leadership as father starts from him pursuing an intimate relationship with and being submissive to God, our heavenly father. This enables him to have and apply God's practical wisdom in all areas of his life.

CHAPTER 8

YES, YOU CAN OVERCOME AND BE FREE FROM VIOLENCE, ANGER AND ABUSE

Family violence is when someone who has a close personal relationship with you harms you, controls you, or makes you feel afraid. The violence may not always be physical but can be emotional or psychological, and create just as much harm. It is not your fault. It is the abuser who is responsible. Family violence can happen to anyone in any neighbourhood or group. Family violence hurts families, communities, and individuals. Everyone has the right to be safe and not live in fear. There is help for you to be safe. In family violence, the abusive person could be anyone significant to you, such as your current or past partner, child, brother or sister, parent, cousin, grandparent, someone you are caring for or who cares for you, or perhaps someone you have a kinship or cultural duty towards. Domestic violence, child abuse, parent abuse, and elder abuse are all part of family violence. Physical harm, rape or sexual abuse, damaging property, harming pets, stalking, and threats to injure or kill are criminal offences. Other forms of family violence that are also damaging include emotional and psychological abuse; put downs and humiliation, social abuse; controlling where you go and who you see; financial abuse; unfairly controlling money; and threats of violence, including threats of self-harm. Other forms of abuse include controlling your spiritual or cultural choices, and blaming you for not fixing family and community problems.

WHAT ARE THE EFFECTS OF FAMILY VIOLENCE?

Abuse in families has serious consequences.

For the family, children will show signs of distress, anger, or self-blame; there will be household conflict and a breakdown in family functioning; frequent moving to avoid the abuser; child protection or police involvement.

For the wider community, it causes children to grow up without learning about positive, respectful relationships; it causes community conflict; abusers go to prison; there are feelings of collective shame and despair, and higher rates of drug and alcohol use and mental health problems.

For the victim, it causes fear, depression, shame and anger, use of drugs or alcohol to block out the pain, physical health problems, being suicidal, and injury, or at the extreme, death. If you or someone you know is experiencing any of these abuses, or if you recognise that you are harming, frightening, or controlling someone close to you, GET HELP IMMEDIATELY.

WHAT CAN I DO?

Act now to get help. Remember, the violence is not your fault, and you don't have to put up with it. Everyone has the right to respectful, loving family relationships, and no one should live in fear. Talk to someone who is safe—do not try coping alone; make contact with a family and domestic violence support service; make a safety plan in case you have to escape quickly; see a doctor if you have been injured or you feel anxious or depressed, and get free legal advice from Legal Aid. For immediate help if you are in danger, call the police. If someone you know is experiencing family violence, listen to them. Show them your support, and help them contact a family violence service.

ANGER AND ABUSE

Anger and abuse victims of trauma experience severe violations of personal boundaries. Consequently, persistent anger and anger management problems are common characteristics of individuals who have experienced traumatic events. This is true for survivors of abuse, as well as for survivors of other types of adverse incidents. If loss occurs, anger as a stage of grieving is a common response as well.

Physical, emotional, or sexual abuse in childhood can interrupt the normal development of skills needed for healthy emotional management and relationship building. Consequently, abused children may need to learn age-appropriate interpersonal boundaries, assertiveness, and coping strategies for strong emotions since they learnt the emotional management skills modelled by the abusive adults in their lives. Angry, aggressive, and abusive adults demonstrate disregard of the emotional, psychological, and physical boundaries of others. Children exposed to such behaviour learn that anger and aggression can be used in relationships to communicate, establish dominance, exert control, solve problems, and resolve conflict.

Another significant source of anger for adults who were abused as children is the deep sense of betrayal and abandonment experienced during childhood abuse. Children look to significant adults in their lives for protective nurturance. Frustration is a normal response to having unmet dependency needs. Chronic frustration, as in situations of prolonged or frequent abuse, will typically develop into chronic anger. Additionally, revenge fantasies often fuel chronic anger management problems for victims of childhood abuse. Revenge fantasies also play a significant role in anger problems related to abuse situations in later life.

In domestic violence, victims of domestic violence experience many personal violations during the abusive relationship. These include the violation of physical boundaries in battering, as well as the violation of emotional, mental, and psychological boundaries caused by *hands-off* abuse. Power, control, and manipulation tactics used in intimate partner violence place victims in situations of constant scrutiny, monitoring, submissiveness, and fear. Such circumstances create a *survival* response in victims. Anger is a common and natural part of such an experience. It is an instinctive response to violation and danger.

Additionally, power and control dynamics in domestic violence perpetuate rigid relationship roles of domination and submission. A typical response to prolonged submission created by abuse is a desire to gain dominance over the aggressor. Some victims of domestic violence become *mutually* aggressive in incidents of battering as a reaction to having been victimised. Others become aggressive in a retaliatory way, waiting for opportunities to victimise their abusers. Still, others will become aggressive in relationships in order to *protect* themselves from potential abusers.

Individuals who must cope with persisting symptoms of trauma-induced strain will typically have less resilient response to any new stress added by living ordinary lives in which ordinary problems arise. Frustration, impatience, irritability, anxiety, and cumulative stress can trigger angry outbursts and even aggression. Without good stress management techniques built into everyday life, stress and poor coping continue and complicate each new life challenge. For many living with poor stress management habits, anger and aggression are frequently used in an attempt to *blow off steam*, gain control, resolve conflicts, or solve problems.

Distressed caregivers and individuals who work in highly stressful situations for prolonged periods are at risk of trauma and related anger problems. Coping skills are taxed by insufficient recuperation time, other forms of poor self-care, and accumulating stress. Healthcare professionals and emergency responders exemplify the types of professionals who often work in such situations. *Burnout* is a common occupational hazard for them.

Regular and effective stress management practices are necessary to prevent inappropriate emotionality during job burnout and in other situations of over-responsibility. Caring for loved ones that are debilitated for long periods of time, for example, can create the same *on-the-job* dynamics of inadequate stress management and poor coping. For individuals who are also survivors of trauma, burnout and fatigue can dramatically compound the risk of anger management problems.

ABUSIVE ANGER

Abusive anger benefits abusive people by sending shockwaves of doubt and fear through their target's mind and body. The target will freeze, flee, or fight back. The best thing to do is flee— leave the area. Besides preventing further emotional turmoil, abusive anger can turn violent even if the abuser has never physically assaulted anyone. During anger attacks, the abuser will tell their victim that they are horrible bits of trash that do not deserve to live, and despite the abuser's craziness, the victims begin to feel that they are somehow *wrong,* and seek to calm the abuser. If you've been in an abusive relationship long enough to get used to your partner's anger, then it's likely you will not feel appropriately fearful as other people would. You become accustomed to the yelling, raging, stomping, swearing, banging on walls, breaking things and irrational fit throwing; but if a friend were to witness the same event, she or he would feel violated, angry, and afraid of the abuser's temper.

HOW TO REACT TO ABUSIVE ANGER

The best, and most difficult, reaction is to walk away from the *baby* throwing the tantrum. If the abuser wants to rage and squeal, they can certainly do it without your help. Abusive anger is only a show. Research shows that the abuser's heart rates actually slow down when they rage. Your abuser is psychologically and emotionally calmer when they're acting like a fool. This shows that they did NOT lose control, they do NOT need to be calmed, and you did NOTHING to provoke this anger! If you cannot walk away, you must revert to what you know about your abuser. Do they want you to agree with them? Be silent? Argue back? The answer to all of these questions is, "Yes, they do." They want to escalate the abuse, and all of those reactions show that the abuser is getting to you. Your abuser knows that if they can *get to you*—if they can knock you off balance—then they're going to win, or weaken your defences so they can insert their ideas into your head or cause such emotional upheaval that you're willing to accept anything they say, as long as *it's over!* So, play along. What you say to the abuser when you're stuck in place doesn't matter if you protect your mind. Remind yourself that you're only saying what you need to say to stop the abuse. Play your part just like an actor plays theirs. Do not let the anger get to you—not to the inside you. Detach from the anger, and do what you need to do to make the abuser feel like they've won, if you cannot leave the situation.

THE DIFFERENCE BETWEEN ANGER AND ABUSE

Anger can result in rage, put-downs, and violent acts. Anger is an aversive state ranging from annoyance to rage. Anger is a strong feeling of displeasure and antagonism or indignation. It's an automatic reaction to any real or imagined insult, frustration, or injustice. When someone puts you down, your initial feelings of humiliation are turned into anger—an emotional reaction needing to be expressed. So, anger is ultimately a combination of physiological, emotional, and cognitive responses to certain triggers. In contrast, domestic abuse generally occurs within intimate relationships. Domestic abuse or violence is a pattern of physical and psychological abuse, threats, intimidation, isolation, or economic coercion used by one person to exert power and control over another person in the context of a dating, family, or household relationship. Conversely, anger is an emotion that can be expressed in healthy behaviours, such as assertiveness, problem-solving, negotiation, conflict management, empathy, etc. So, you see that not all anger is wrong. Anger is a problem when it is too frequent, too intense, lasts too long, leads to aggression, and disturbs work or relationships.

DOMESTIC ABUSE AND BATTERING

Battering is a pattern of behaviour that often uses the threat of, or the use of, violence. One person believes they are entitled to control another. Assault, battering, and domestic violence are crimes. In *Why Men Batter Women*, John Gottman and Neil Jacobson write, *"Battering is physical aggression with a purpose: that purpose is to control, intimidate, and subjugate another human being. Battering is always accompanied by emotional abuse, is often accompanied by injury, and is virtually always associated with fear and even terror on the part of the battered woman."* Abuse is always a problem. In fact, there is no excuse for abuse! Why? Because abuse seeks to denigrate, control, or destroy another person!

The abuser's physical attacks or aggressive behaviour can range from bruising to murder. It often begins with what is excused as trivial contacts, which escalate into more frequent and serious attacks.

Sexual abuse and violence, wherein the woman is forced to have sexual intercourse with her abuser or take part in unwanted sexual activity, could accompany the abuser's physical attack.

Psychological battering is an abuser's psychological or mental violence, and can include constant verbal abuse, harassment, excessive possessiveness, isolating the woman from friends and family, deprivation of physical and economic resources, and destruction of personal property.

I believe that emotional breakdown, lack, frustration, anger, having suffered abuse, fear of the unknown, abuse of power, inferiority complex, insecurity, disappointment, discouragement, weakness, infidelity, the influence of drugs, and any negative influence of negative family members and friends, could make a man or a woman be abusive or violent to their partner. I believe there are solutions to these issues in relationships. Such a person should realise and admit that they have a problem, and they should seek help such as professional counselling, pastoral counselling, and support, prayer, and/or spiritual deliverance with the help of a pastor. They should also have the willingness to help others by sharing their testimony after they have overcome the problem. With God, all things are possible, and there is nothing too difficult for God of the Universe to do.

IN THE NEXT CHAPTER

In the next chapter, we will discover what forgiveness is, and how to forgive and emotionally forget quickly. Forgiveness and being able to emotionally forget will reflect in your emotions and give you peace, joy, and success.

CHAPTER 9

YES, YOU CAN FORGIVE YOURSELF
AND FORGIVE OTHERS

Permit me to share my story before we go further in this chapter. My life experience was full of shame, neglect, abandonment, rejection, isolation, and on top of this, I was physically, sexually, and verbally abused constantly by family, relatives, and friends. I lost my identity, my position in the family, respect from siblings and others, my dignity, and my voice. All the negative words said to me and against me followed me for years, and I believed it and said it to myself for years. I had low self-esteem and lacked boldness and confidence. I eventually believed it myself that I was a nobody. I was afraid to do anything—to stand in front of people, to lead or to speak out in public. I kept everything to myself and was very afraid before I got married. I actually wanted to stay single and not get married at all. However, I entered into relationship with all the emotional trauma, and instead of things getting better, it got worse; that is, until I started to deal with the situation in order to turn a negative situation around to a positive one.

MY EARLY CHILDHOOD

I was born in the UK, and then, at the age of three, my parents took me to Nigeria to live with my relatives and to go to school there. However, the period of living miles away from my parents at such an early age was a traumatic experience. While my parents were still living in Europe, they had other children, and it was unknown to me for a long time that I had two other sisters. In fact, I completely forgot who my parents were. I could not recognise them when they returned. During those seven years of terrible experience of no father, no mother, and no relative to show up in my junior school, I started experiencing emotions of anger, frustration, loneliness, and rejection, and feelings of being abandoned; and I was abused. There were times I was so hungry and thirsty that I was begging my friends at school for snacks, and even picking up crumbs of biscuits or food from the floor. As a result, I often ended up eating unpleasant things from the floor. The scar on part of my body was also such that I was ashamed of bathing in a public bathroom or swimming like others. As a little five or six-year-old girl, I would say that my father and mother were in heaven, pointing to the sky.

One particular year when the owner of the school realised my school fees had mounted up and nothing had been paid for a long time, they decided to return some students, who owed school fees, to their parents. These included me, and they took us all with the school mini bus and travelled around locating the parents in different places. After hours of travelling and trying to locate where my relatives lived, it was still not successful, and the driver of the school bus brought me back alone to the school premises. The driver of the bus, knowing the child was helpless, and with no one around, parked and raped the child, took advantage of her, stole her pride, and damaged her innocence. This created terrible self-esteem in a six-year-old.

He had told me not to tell anyone, and so I kept quiet about it until adulthood, when I decided to break out and write this book.

Some years later, a relative eventually showed up at school and took me to visit another family. Unknown to me, I was about to meet my biological mum for the first time since age 3 years. During my stay with this relative, there was this woman with her Afro hair style, cute red trousers and blouse, with high heels and beautiful makeup and lovely jewellery. I could not believe anyone could be living in such a comfortable lifestyle. I wished to myself that she was my mother. I also whispered it to grandma. I eventually discovered she was my mother. She had come back from Europe to live permanently in Africa, and wanted my brother and I to come live with her and our two younger sisters. It was then I discovered that the boy I had seen around so many times at some relation's house was actually my brother.

However, the relationship wasn't there—no love and no dignity and no respect. The bridge was too wide; the gap was big. Emotions were broken and damaged between my brother, my sisters, our parent, and myself—no faith, no love, no hope, and no trust. The two younger sisters from Europe could not relate with the older siblings properly, and the parent did not help either but practised favouritism instead. I felt disliked, hated, and disrespected among family, close relatives, and friends.

This book is to enable you to see that you can overcome negative experiences, that you can prove negative words and negative opinions of others wrong, and turn such negativity into positivity. I have been there, stayed in it, and I have been able to overcome it; and if you are in it, you can overcome it too.

NEGATIVE EXPERIENCES, EMOTIONAL WOUNDS AND FORGIVENESS

Negative experiences and emotional wounds can leave you with lasting feelings of anger, bitterness, or even vengeance. But if you don't practice forgiveness, you might be the one who pays most dearly, as the cycle of pain, hurt, and unforgiveness continue. By embracing forgiveness, you can also embrace peace, hope, gratitude, and joy. Consider how forgiveness can lead you to physical, emotional, and spiritual healing and well-being.

Forgiveness doesn't mean that you excuse the other person's inappropriate behaviour, and it doesn't minimise or justify the wrong. You can forgive the person without excusing the act. Forgiveness brings a kind of peace that helps you go on with life.

Forgiving others is essential for spiritual growth. Your experience of someone who has hurt you, while painful, is now a thought or feeling that you carry around. These thoughts of resentment, anger, and hatred represent slow, debilitating energies that will dis-empower you if you continue to let these thoughts occupy space in your head. If you could release them, you would know more peace. Release all those negative thoughts from you. Turn your hurts over to God, and allow the Spirit to flow through you. Reconnect to Spirit—make a new agreement with yourself to always stay connected to Spirit, even when it seems to be the most difficult thing to do. If you do this, you will allow whatever degree of perfect harmony that your body was designed for, to proliferate. Your new agreement with reality, in which you've blended your physical self and your personality with your spiritual God-connected self, will begin to radiate a higher energy of love and light. Wherever you go, others will experience the glow of your God consciousness, and disharmony and disorder and all manner of problems simply will not flourish in your presence. Become "an instrument of thy peace," as St. Francis desires in the first line of his famous prayer.

Forgiving and forgetting is a skill that requires work to become good at it. But be smart. If someone took advantage of you, it doesn't mean you shouldn't be careful to prevent it from happening again. Forgiving means that you should let it go so you don't have to be miserable thinking about that person every day for the next 5 years. Negative emotions are tools that can tell us that something might be wrong. For your best results, take the appropriate action at the time something happens, and then be done with the emotion. Forgive and move on with your life! Nearly everyone has been hurt by the actions or words of another. Perhaps your mother criticised your parenting skills, or your work colleague sabotaged a project, or your partner had an affair. Generally, forgiveness is a decision to let go of resentment and thoughts of revenge. The act that hurt or offended you might always remain a part of your life, but forgiveness can lessen its grip on you and help you focus on other, more positive parts of your life. Forgiveness can even lead to feelings of understanding, empathy, and compassion for the one who hurt you.

What Are the Benefits of Forgiving Someone?

Letting go of grudges and bitterness can make way for happiness, health, and peace. Forgiveness can lead to healthier relationships, greater spiritual and psychological well-being, less anxiety, less stress and hostility, lower blood pressure, fewer symptoms of depression, a stronger immune system, improved heart health, and higher self-esteem.

Why Is It So Easy to Hold a Grudge?

When someone you love and trust hurts you, you might become angry, sad, or confused. If you dwell on hurtful events or situations, grudges filled with resentment, vengeance, and hostility can take root. If you allow negative feelings to crowd out positive feelings, you might find yourself swallowed up by your own bitterness or sense of injustice.

What Are the Effects of Holding a Grudge?

If you're unforgiving, you might bring anger and bitterness into every relationship, and into new experiences; you might become so wrapped up in the wrong that you can't enjoy the present; you might become depressed or anxious, and feel that your life lacks meaning or purpose, or that you're at odds with your spiritual beliefs; you might lose valuable and enriching connectedness with others.

A LESSON IN UNFORGIVENESS

This is a story Jesus told in the Bible. Once upon a time, there was a king who wished to settle accounts with his servants. When he began the accounting, one who owed him 10,000 talents was brought to him. However, he could not repay, so his master ordered him to be sold, with his wife and his children and everything that he possessed, and payment to be made. The servant fell on his knees and begged him, saying, "Have patience with me and I will repay you everything." And his master's heart was moved with compassion, and he released him and forgave him [cancelling] the debt. However, that same servant went out and found one of his fellow servants who owed him a hundred denarii; and he seized him and began choking him, saying, "Pay what you owe!" So, his fellow servant fell on his knees and begged him earnestly, "Have patience with me and I will repay you." But he was unwilling, and he went and had him thrown in prison until he paid back the debt. When his fellow servants saw what had happened, they were deeply grieved, and they went and reported to their master [with clarity and in detail] everything that had taken place. Then his master called him and said to him, "You wicked and contemptible slave. I forgave all that [great] debt of yours because you begged me. Should you not have had mercy on your fellow slave [who owed you little by comparison], as I had mercy on you?" And in wrath, his master turned him over to the torturers (jailers) until he paid all that he owed. Jesus then said, "My heavenly Father will also do the same to [every one of] you, if each of you does not forgive his brother from your heart."

HOW CAN I FORGIVE AND BE FREE?

To begin, consider the value of forgiveness and its importance in your life at a given time; reflect on the facts of the situation, how it has affected your life, health, and well-being. Forgiveness will help you move away from your role as victim and release the control and power that the offending person and situation have had on your life, and as you let go of grudges, you'll no longer define your life by how you've been hurt.

Unforgiveness is the root of bitterness; it robs us of the full life God intends for us. Rather than promote justice, our unforgiveness festers into bitterness. Hebrews 12:14–15 warns, "Make every effort to live in peace with everyone and to be holy; without holiness, no one will see the Lord. See to it that no one falls short of the grace of God, and that no bitter root rises up to cause trouble and defile many." Similarly, 2 Corinthians 2:5–11 warns that unforgiveness can be an opening for Satan to derail us. If you have resentment against someone else, use this time to forgive him or her. Learn to forgive and forget quickly. It will reflect in your emotions and give you peace and joy. Identify what happened, identify what it caused you, tell God what happened, and release the hurt caused by the offender to the court of God, which is scary for the offender. Now they have to answer to God, a much Higher Court, because forgiveness does not let the offender off the hook! It just releases you from the burden of carrying it, and so it is for your good. Tell the offender you have chosen to forgive—which is the process of releasing the matter to God's jurisdiction.

Forgiving someone does not mean the offence or hurt didn't happen. Forgiveness doesn't necessarily resume trust. I know through experience that when we choose to forgive and allow that to work within our hearts, doing away with anger, hurt, bitterness, fear, thoughts of self-pity or self-righteousness, then the event becomes nothing but a memory. We are able to bless those who have injured us, with a sincere heart, and are even willing to return to the relationship if it is safe to do so. This way, if it is a relationship that God needs for us to get back into, we can build again what God intended to build the first time before the offence happened. Some of your healing and miracle requires your forgiveness to yourself and to others. Let the offence go, and let your miracle come in. Forgiveness lets you turn your back to bitterness. If you have a regret about something you've done, use this moment to forgive yourself. If you have resentment against someone else, use this time to forgive him or her.

Forgiveness is a commitment to a process of change. The remaining sections of this chapter is devoted to helping you to further understand forgiveness, and how to stay in a state of forgiveness.

Don't Go to Sleep Angry

Each night as I drift off to sleep, I adamantly refuse to use this precious time to review anything that I do not want reinforced in the hours of being immersed in my subconscious mind. I choose to impress upon my subconscious mind my conception of myself in alignment with God. I reiterate my "I am," which I have placed in my imagination, and I remember that my slumber will be dominated by my last waking concept of myself. I am peaceful, I am content, I am love, and I attract only to myself those who are in alignment with my highest ideals of myself. This is my nightly ritual, always eschewing any temptation to go over any fear of unpleasantness that my ego might be asking me to review. I assume the feeling in my body of those "I am" statements already fulfilled, and I know that I'm allowing myself to be programmed while asleep, for the next day I rise knowing that I am God's wonderful creation and his workmanship created unto good works.

> *"In sleep, man impresses the subconscious mind*
> *with his conception of himself."*
> – Neville Goddard

Switch the Focus from Blaming Others to Understanding Yourself

Whenever you're upset over the conduct of others, take the focus off those you're holding responsible for your inner distress. Shift your mental energy to allowing yourself to be with whatever you're feeling—let the experience be as it may, without blaming others for your feelings. Don't blame yourself either! Just allow the experience to unfold, and tell yourself that no one has the power to make you uneasy, without your consent, and that you're unwilling to grant that authority to this person right now. Tell yourself that you are willing to freely experience your emotions without calling them *wrong*, or needing to chase them away. In this way, you've made a shift to self-mastery. It's important to bypass blame, and even to bypass your desire to understand the other person; instead, focus on understanding yourself. By taking responsibility for how you choose to respond to anything or anyone, you're aligning yourself with the beautiful dance of life. By changing the way you choose to perceive the power that others have over you, you will see a bright new world of unlimited potential for yourself, and you will know instantly how to forgive and let go of anything.

Avoid Telling People What to Do

Avoid thoughts and activities that involve telling people, who are perfectly capable of making their own choices, what to do. In your family, remember that you do not own anyone. In fact, disregard any inclination to dominate in all of your relationships. Listen rather than expound. Pay attention to yourself when you're having judgmental opinions, and see where self-attention takes you. You should replace an ownership mentality with one of allowing so that you are free of frustration with those who don't behave according to your ego-dominated expectations.

Take Responsibility for Your Part

Removing blame means never assigning responsibility to anyone else for what you're experiencing. If you take responsibility for having the experience, then at least you have a chance to also take responsibility for removing it or learning from it. If you're in some small (perhaps unknown) way responsible for that migraine headache or that depressed feeling, then you can go to work to remove it. If, on the other hand, someone or something else is responsible in your mind, then of course you'll have to wait until they change for you to get better. And that is unlikely to occur. So, you go home with nothing, and are left with nothing, when peace is really on the other side of the coin.

Let Go of Resentments

What causes annoyance and anger after a dispute? The generic response would be a laundry list detailing why the other person was wrong and how illogically and unreasonably they behaved, concluding with something like, "I have a right to be upset when my [daughter, mother-in law, ex-husband, boss, or whomever you're thinking of] speaks to me that way!" Resentments don't come from the conduct of the other party in an altercation—no, they survive and thrive because you're unwilling to end that altercation with an offering of kindness, love, and authentic forgiveness. Someone must risk returning injury with kindness, or hostility will never turn to goodwill. So, when all of the yelling, screaming, and threatening words have been expressed, the time for calm has arrived. Remember that no storm lasts forever, and that hidden within are always seeds of tranquillity. There is a time for hostility and a time for peace.

Be Kind Instead Of Right

There is a Chinese proverb that says, "If you're going to pursue revenge, you'd better dig two graves." This means your resentments will destroy you. The world is just the way it is. The people who are behaving *badly* in the world are doing what they're supposed to be doing. You can process it in any way that you choose. If you're filled with anger about all of those *problems*, you are one more person who contributes to the pollution of anger. Instead, remember that you have no need to make others wrong or to retaliate when you've been wronged. Imagine if someone says something to you that you find offensive, and rather than opting for resentment, you learn to depersonalise what you've just heard and respond with kindness. You are willing to freely send the higher, faster energies of love, peace, joy, forgiveness, and kindness as your response to whatever comes your way. You do this for yourself. You would rather be kind than right.

Practice Giving

Amidst arguments and disagreements, practice giving rather than taking before you exit. Giving involves leaving the ego behind. While it wants to win and show its superiority by being contrary and disrespectful, you should act to be at peace and live in harmony. Wherever you are, whenever you feel strong emotions stirring in you, and you notice yourself feeling the need to *be right*, silently recite the following words from the Prayer of Saint Francis: "Where there is injury, [let me bring] pardon. Let me bring love to hate, light to darkness, and pardon to injury." You can reduce your quarrelling time to almost zero if you practice this procedure. Read these words daily, for they'll help you overcome your ego's demands, and to know the fullness of life.

Stop Looking for Occasions to Be Offended

When you live at or below ordinary levels of awareness, you spend a great deal of time and energy finding opportunities to be offended. A news report, a rude stranger, someone cursing, a sneeze, a black cloud—just about anything will do if you're looking for an occasion to be offended. Become a person who refuses to be offended by any one, anything, or any set of circumstances. If you have enough faith in your own beliefs, you'll find that it's impossible to be offended by the beliefs and conduct of others. Not being offended is a way of saying: "I have control over how I'm going to feel, and I choose to feel peaceful regardless of what I observe going on." When you feel offended, you're practicing judgment. You judge someone else to be stupid, insensitive, rude, arrogant, inconsiderate, or foolish, and then you find yourself upset and offended by their conduct. What you may not realise is that, when you judge another person, you do not define them. You define yourself as someone who needs to judge others.

Don't Live in the Past

When we find it difficult to forgive, often it is because we are not living in the present, but instead, we are assigning more importance to the past. Sometimes we assign a good portion of our energy and attention lamenting the good old days that are gone forever, and we say things like, "Everything has changed;" "No one respects anyone else like they used to..." etc. This is assigning responsibility to the past for why you can't be happy and fulfilled today. Though humans are higher intelligent and thinking beings than other mammals, we can still learn a thing or 2 from other creatures of God, such as a beaver. A beaver only does beaver, and he does it right in the moment. He doesn't spend his days ruminating over the fact that his beaver siblings received more attention, or his father beaver ran off with a younger beaver when he was growing up. He's always in the now. We should enjoy the present moment rather than using it up consumed with anger over the past or worry about the future.

Embrace Your Dark Times

As tough as it is to acknowledge, you had to go through what you went through in order to get to where you are today, and the evidence is that you did. Every spiritual advance that you will make in your life will very likely be preceded by what you might consider unpleasant. Those dark times, tough episodes, break ups, periods of impoverishment, illnesses, abuses, and broken dreams were all in order. They happened, so you can assume they had to, and embrace them from that perspective, and then understand them, accept them, honour them, and finally transform them.

Refrain from Judgement

When you stop judging and simply become an observer, you will know inner peace. With that sense of inner peace, you'll find yourself happier and free of the negative energy of resentment. A bonus is that you'll find that others are much more attracted to you. A peaceful person attracts peaceful energy. If I'm to be a being of love living from my highest self, then that means that love is all I have inside of me, and all that I have to give away. If someone I love chooses to be something other than what my ego would prefer, I must send them the ingredients of my highest self, which is God, and God is love, and my criticism and condemnation of the thoughts, feelings, and behaviour of others—regardless of how right and moral my human-self convinces me it is—is a step away from God-realisation. It is God-consciousness that allows for my wishes to be fulfilled, as long as they are aligned with my Source of being. I can come up with a long list of reasons why I should be judgmental and condemnatory toward another of God's children and why I am right. Yet, if I want to perfect my own world—and I so want to do so—then I must substitute love for these judgments.

Send Love

When we are steadfast and we never slip in our abstention from thoughts of harm directed toward others, then all living creatures cease to feel enmity in our presence. Now, I know that we are all human: you, me, all of us. We do occasionally slip and retreat from our highest self into judgment, criticism, and condemnation, but this is not a rationale for choosing to practice that kind of interaction. I can only tell you that when I finally got it, and I sent only love to another of God's children whom I had been judging and criticising, I got the immediate result of inner contentment. I urge you to send love in place of those judgments and criticisms to others when you feel they impede your joy and happiness, and hold them in that place of love. Notice that if you stay steadfast, when you change the way you look at things, the things you look at change. Picture yourself at the termination of a quarrel or major dispute. Rather than reacting with old patterns of residual anger, revenge, and hurt, visualise offering kindness, love, and forgiveness. Do this right now by sending out these *true virtue* thoughts regarding any resentment you're currently carrying. Make this your standard response to any future altercations: I end on love, no matter what!

Commit to Letting Go

It's difficult to accomplish anything without having the intention of doing so. Most people don't miraculously lose 25 pounds or accidentally start saving an extra £100 every month; anything positive normally starts with an intention. So, commit to finding a way to forgive and move on. You have a choice. You are an intelligent, thoughtful creature. We don't have to simply react to things like lower animals. You do have a choice about how you interpret things and the actions you take afterwards. You can also change your mind and choose something different after your initial reaction. You can choose. Be empathetic. It's easy to just assume that the other person is just a bad person, but maybe there is more to it than that. What else do they have going on in their lives? Has something happened in their past that caused them to behave the way that they did? Try to see things from their perspective. You might be surprised by what you find.

Consider your part in it. Did you contribute to the issue in some way? It's rare that anyone is 100% innocent when a disagreement occurs. Realising your part in the matter can help you understand their motivation. Also, it's important to find forgiveness for yourself as well, if you regret anything that you did or said. Focus on the here and now. Constantly reliving the past just keeps the hurt feelings churning. One of the keys to life is to be in the present. Look around you; what do you see? What are you doing? If you're washing the dishes, be 100% aware of the fact that you're washing the dishes, not thinking about other things. Be present. Move on. Forgive the person and you'll immediately feel better. We are at our best when we act with compassion. We feel great, too, when compassion and forgiveness are automatically part of our lives. Forgiveness is something that you largely do for yourself.

It may be very difficult to forgive someone. Forgiveness can be challenging, especially if the person who's hurt you doesn't admit wrong or doesn't speak of his or her sorrow. If you find yourself stuck, consider the situation from the other person's point of view, and ask yourself why he or she would behave in such a way. Perhaps you would have reacted similarly if you faced the same situation. Reflect on times you've hurt others and on those who've forgiven you. Write in a journal, pray, or use guided meditation. You can also talk with a person you've found to be wise and compassionate, such as a spiritual leader, a mental health provider, or an impartial loved one or friend. Be aware that forgiveness is a process, and even small hurts may need to be revisited and forgiven over and over again.

You may ask, what if the person I'm forgiving doesn't change? Getting another person to change his or her actions, behaviour, or words isn't the point of forgiveness. Think of forgiveness more about how it can change your life—by bringing you peace, happiness, and emotional and spiritual healing. Forgiveness can take away the power the other person continues to wield in your life.

DOES FORGIVENESS GUARANTEE RECONCILIATION?

If the hurtful event involved someone whose relationship you otherwise value, forgiveness can lead to reconciliation. This, however, isn't always the case. Reconciliation might be impossible if the offender has died or is unwilling to communicate with you. In other cases, reconciliation might not be appropriate. Still, forgiveness is possible—even if reconciliation isn't.

Having to interact with the person who hurt you may be difficult. If you haven't reached a state of forgiveness, being near the person who hurt you might prompt you to be tense and stressful. To handle these situations, remember that you can choose to attend or avoid specific functions and gatherings. If you choose to attend, don't be surprised by a certain amount of awkwardness and perhaps even more intense feelings. Respect yourself and do what seems best, doing your best to keep an open mind. You might find that the experience helps you to move forward with forgiveness.

WHEN IT'S YOU WHO NEEDS FORGIVENESS

The first step is to honestly assess and acknowledge the wrongs you've done and how those wrongs have affected others. At the same time, avoid judging yourself too harshly. You're human, and you'll make mistakes. If you're truly sorry for something you've said or done, consider admitting it to those you've harmed. Speak of your sincere sorrow or regret, and specifically ask for forgiveness, without making excuses. Remember, however, you can't force someone to forgive you. Others need to move to forgiveness in their own time. Whatever the outcome, commit to treating others with compassion, empathy, and respect.

In conclusion of this chapter, everyone has suffered some sort of emotional hurt through the words or actions of another. Experiencing this hurt is completely natural, but sometimes the hurt lasts longer than it needs to. This makes it harder to be happy and, if we can't let go and move on, it can ruin relationships. Someone that can never forgive is someone destined to be alone. Forgiveness is one of the ways you can profoundly change your life. It's not always easy, but it's a skill that can be learned. It just takes practice.

IN THE NEXT CHAPTER

I cannot finish this book without adding a most important chapter on Yes, You Can Love Again. So, in this next chapter, we look at Love, the meaning of Love, and how Love helps us in our journey of success.

CHAPTER 10

YES, YOU CAN LOVE AGAIN

Love (L – Listen, O – Overcome, V – Value, E – Empower) is my own personal and practical way that has helped me in my journey of success. Love is the background and foundation of my marriage and relationships. Whenever I faced challenges, I always reminded myself of what love is, and this strengthens my relationships. Love has kept me strong. Love is a profoundly tender, passionate affection for another person, a feeling of warm personal attachment or deep affection… (as defined by Explore Dictionary.com). Love can also be a virtue representing human kindness, compassion, and affection, as *"the unselfish, loyal, and benevolent concern for the good of another."*

LOVE…A MORE EXCELLENT WAY OF LIFE

The following is an exposition of God's kind of love from the Bible, 1 Corinthians, Chapter 13:

Love always protects (defends, guards, shields). Love protects the relationship with loved ones. Love protects and shields loved ones from harm or hurt. Love also protects loved ones from self-harm through correction in love. Love defends loved ones regardless of whether they are present or not.

Love always trusts (believes, is convinced). Love trusts and believes in a future that is good for one's self and for the loved ones. Love trusts the loved ones in spite of present unsteady conditions, and is convinced of a better future for the loved ones.

Love is always hopeful (confident, expectant, optimistic). Love hopes for the better from and for the beloved, and confidently expects things to turn out good for both self and for beloved, and is very optimistic about the future for the beloved.

Love always preserves (persists, continues, sticks with, endures). Love perseveres for the beloved, patiently waiting for good works no matter what. Love continues to wait in expectation of good, enduring the pain of the moment.

Love endures with patience and serenity; love is kind and thoughtful; love is not jealous or envious; love does not brag and is not proud or arrogant. Love is not rude; it is not self-seeking; it is not easily provoked (nor overly sensitive and easily angered); it does not take into account a wrong endured.

Love bears all things (regardless of what comes), believes all things (looking for the best in each one), hopes all things (remaining steadfast during difficult times) and endures all things without weakening.

Love never gives up. Love cares more for others than for self. Love doesn't want what it doesn't have.

Love doesn't strut, doesn't have a swelled head, doesn't force itself on others, and isn't always "me first." Love doesn't fly off the handle, doesn't keep score of the sins of others, doesn't revel when others grovel, takes pleasure in the flowering of truth, puts up with anything, trusts God always, always looks for the best, never looks back, but keeps going to the end.

Love never dies. Inspired speech will be over some day; praying in tongues will end; understanding will reach its limit. We know only a portion of the truth, and what we say about God is always incomplete. But when the Complete arrives, our incomplete will be cancelled.

DIFFERENT KINDS OF LOVE

As earlier discussed, according to Explore Dictionary.com, love is a profoundly tender, passionate affection for another person; a feeling of warm personal attachment or deep affection as for a parent, child, or friend, etc. It could also be sexual passion or desire. Love encompasses a variety of different emotional and mental states, typically strong and positively experienced, ranging from the most sublime virtue or good habit, the simplest pleasure to the deepest interpersonal affection. For example, the love of a mother differs from the love of a spouse, which differs from the love of food. Most commonly, love refers to a feeling of strong attraction and emotional attachment. Love is also a virtue representing human kindness, compassion, and affection. It may also describe caring actions towards one's self, other humans, or animals.

QUESTIONS AND ANSWERS FOR LOVE AND RELATIONSHIPS

Why Do We Need Good Relationships?

Human beings are naturally very sociable. We enjoy the company of others and crave positive interactions and meaningful friendships. To some extent, good relationships are just as important for our survival as food and water, and this can explain why our health and happiness suffer when our relationships go wrong. Therefore, the better our relationships work, the happier and healthier we are going to be. Extensive research has shown that people with satisfying relationships are likely to have fewer health problems and live longer. In contrast, those who do not have many social connections tend to show signs of depression and cognitive decline.

What Defines A Good Relationship?

All relationships are unique, but there are several characteristics that can signify strong, healthy connections, such as relationships that are built on trust, which is essential for good communication and forming strong bonds. Without trust, relationships are unlikely to survive. Being mindful of what you do and say means you are more likely to maintain strong relationships. Relationship issues can arise if you let your negative emotions affect others. Strong, supportive relationships rely heavily on mutual respect, as it fosters understanding of each other's needs and values. Relationships will be richer if you make an effort to keep in contact with those around you, and being honest and open with others also allows for you to connect deeply and build long-lasting bonds.

How Can I Find the Right Woman or Man?

Indeed, good women are resilient, beautiful, and desirable. This is not to say all women encompass these traits, but a vast majority of them do. For men seeking a serious relationship, it can be hard to discern and ascertain whether a woman is truly *good* (and vice versa). Men of virtue who have been in the dating game for any long period will often accept nothing less; yet many of these same men also lack knowledge about who the *right woman* may be. Discovering a genuine, good-hearted person is the first battle.

While there are exceptions to the rule, most happy couples will say there was a connection of some type at the beginning, and that they felt it quickly. The simple fact is that you can't love someone you're not attracted to. This not only applies to physical appearance but emotional, spiritual, and intellectual as well. Your thought patterns are similar (in most ways). Men in a committed, happy relationship are still taken aback by how frequently their thoughts seem to align with their partner's. Two people meant for each other will often complete each other's sentences. One will bring up a topic that the other was just about to. You won't always agree with each other (a good sign), but that's also part of the fun. Since this article is about finding the right woman or man, here is a useful tip: looks are not nearly as important to a woman as they are to a man. Humour, confidence, charm, charisma, and strength are more important to a woman.

Affection and love grows in time. Following the first couple of dates, one should know whether or not there's *something there.* In the later stages, truly happy couples will reminisce about how their love and affection for one another grew over time. Imperfections are accepted, even embraced. The love and affection you feel for the right woman overcomes everything else. You laugh together a lot. If your relationship lacks humour and laughter, that's usually not a good sign. A mutual sense of humour is among the most important indications of chemistry. For those with an astute sense of humour, the *right* woman will probably make you laugh quite often, and vice versa. If not, she's probably not the right person. There's a mutual, unshakable sense of respect when it's the right person. We are not talking about the type of respect shown to one's boss; nor are we talking about *morality-based* respect. When you've found the right one, and the relationship develops, the love and adoration you have for her will be so entrenched that the last thing you'll ever want to do is hurt her. She highly respects you as a man. You highly respect her as a woman. Both people do so out of love—nothing else. With the right person, your priorities will change. That's what the right person does. You grab each other's hearts, and you both fall in deep love. For both of you, the period of single life that you enjoyed quickly fades from memory. Not only does it fade, but you're so thankful that it has. You both want the same things in life. This last one is so very important. Many relationships that end do so because one wants something the other doesn't; for example, kids, a house, living in a different country, working full-time or staying home, etc. While you won't necessarily want everything the other does, life-changing wants and needs should be mutually agreed upon.

How Can Personal Challenges Be Solved?

Recognise, realise, and admit there is a problem that needs a solution. Seek for help sooner, in the right place and from the right people; for example, professional counselling, pastoral counselling and elder's wisdom. Pray until something happens (PUSH); with mutual agreement, pray together always. Seek support from others but watch who you share your problems with, and avoid bad influences. Spiritual deliverance prayer by a pastor will most likely involve dealing with background issues, past experiences, breaking generational and family curses, and bondages and barriers to get you delivered. Once the problem is solved, be willing to share the testimony and tell your story about how you overcame so that you can help others facing the same challenges. Believe that it is possible, and that there is nothing too difficult for God.

If you have a resentment against someone else, use this time to forgive them. Things don't always go as planned. Learn to forgive and forget quickly. It will reflect in your emotions and give you peace and joy. Hebrews 12:14–15 warns, "Make every effort to live in peace with everyone and to be holy; without holiness, no one will see the Lord. See to it that no one falls short of the grace of God and that no bitter root rises up to cause trouble and defile many."

What Causes Relationship Problems?

There are a number of patterns and situations that can develop within a relationship that will contribute to problems occurring: neglect of the relationship, conflict, poor management of differences between partners, withdrawing care and affection, loss of compassion, and times of crisis. All relationships face difficulties, and most are resolved over time. However, when the problems become entrenched and seem unable to be solved, it is important to seek professional help. It is far better to resolve the problems than to dissolve the relationship. Unfortunately, research shows that the average couple waits six years before seeking help once the problem is recognised, and only a small percentage seek the professional help they need. Half of all marriages that end do so in the first seven years. These statistics are very sad. Both partners would agree that assistance is required to gain a new perspective and to try something different for the relationship to become unstuck, and for mending to occur. However, if your partner is reluctant or unwilling to seek help, then it can be very helpful for you to seek help first. You can't make your partner change, but changes you make can start the domino effect of change for the relationship. It is important that you seek help from someone who is trained and experienced in working with relationships, such as a relationship counsellor. Most people ask friends for recommendations, and word of mouth is a good way to find help. You can also ask your GP for a recommendation. A relationship counsellor will work with couples who are experiencing difficulties, affairs and betrayals, separation, divorce, pre-nuptial issues, family issues, and cross-cultural relationships.

When and Why Should Couples Seek Relationship Counselling, Coaching, and Mentoring?

As soon as possible, couples must seek counselling before and whenever they recognise signs of a problem. In relationship counselling, therapists will work with clients to resolve relationship issues, bearing in mind the above characteristics to explore exactly why things have gone wrong and how problems can be overcome. Relationship counselling, coaching, and mentoring is focused primarily on making sure relationship issues are dealt with in a way that supports the health and wellbeing of those involved. In the workplace, having good relationships with colleagues and others in the professional circle boosts productivity and is valuable for career development. Being on good terms with your boss means you are more likely to be considered if a new position opens up. There is also a sense of freedom to having good relationships. Rather than spending our time and energy overcoming obstacles associated with relationship issues, we are focused on opportunities and personal development.

How Can I Build and Enjoy Intimacy and Sex in Marriage?

Make sexual dynamic a routine part of the relationship, not just intercourse alone, and not just for the sake of making babies, but for intimacy in the marriages. Get creative and keep it exciting, though both of you are bound to eventually lose the sexual urge of the first few months or years of the relationship. While both of you may have a hard time keeping your hands off each other to begin with, now sex may start to feel like a chore. This is a very common problem in relationships, and yet it's one of the easy ones to solve. Always look for new ways to recreate the sexual high of the first few times, and before you know it, both of you may go at it all over again like frisky bunnies.

How Can a Couple Manage Their Time Together?

Do both of you have enough time to spend with each other? These days, time is a luxury that most lovers can't afford. When you start spending too much time away from each other, it's only a matter of time before one of you starts asking the big question, "Do I need my partner in my life anymore?" Don't drift away so far that both of you don't need to be with each other anymore. Find ways to indulge in exciting hobbies, or spend evenings going out on little coffee or ice cream dates. They make for great conversations, and it'll bring both of you closer too. Sharing responsibility, finances, housework, walking the dog, raising the kids, and building a sense of teamwork translates into a sense of interdependence rather than independence, which leads to mutual understanding and a stronger sense of overall connection. As stated by Billy Graham, *"Let us take time to get acquainted with our families. We are not machines. We are not robots. The secret of a happy home is that members of the family learn to give and receive love. Let us take time to express our love in a thousand ways."*

How Can I Trust Rather Than Giving in to Jealousy and Insecurity?

Insecure couples are forever locked in a cycle of jealousy and anger. When you feel jealous about the attention your lover is getting from their recent promotion, you're not helping them become a better individual. It's like a parent who's angry with their child because the child is having *too much fun*. You need to learn to have faith in each other and in the relationship. Instead of letting negativity build inside the relationship, learn to enjoy each other's successes. After all, your partner is your better half, and any accomplishments of theirs are your accomplishments too, aren't they?

How Can I Deal with Incompatibility in Love?

Love at first sight and infatuation can last several months. And it does a good job of masking any differences in a relationship. As perfect as two people may be, sometimes they may just not be perfect for each other. If you find yourself dating someone with whom you have nothing in common, you need to decide on the next step. Try to find common interests that both of you like, or walk your own paths instead of living in frustration.

How Can I Be Contented with Money or Not Enough Money?

Anyone in a relationship for long enough will know just how important money or the lack of it really is. If your friends earn a lot more than you or your partner, it'll end up frustrating both of you. And on the other hand, if both of you earn a lot more than your friends, there'll be a lot of love and happiness in your lives. It's a stupid fact of life. If you're having difficulties in your relationship because of money, perhaps it's time to change your friends and see the difference.

How Can I Understand Change in Priorities?

You may be in a relationship, but that doesn't change who you are. And that's where the problem starts. As individuals, we evolve and change all the time. You're not the person you were last year, and you won't be the person you are now next year. And just like you, your partner too is changing constantly. And every now and then, you and your partner may experience changes that will pull both of you apart from each other. And soon enough, both of you may have nothing in common. Spend enough time with each other, and try to evolve together in a similar direction. Talk about your beliefs and your interests with each other, and it'll help both of you grow together along the same path.

How Can We Give Ourselves Space for Individual Growth?

When you're in a relationship, spending time with each other is very important. But at the same time, spending time away from each other is crucial too. By spending too much time together, you'd subconsciously feel isolated from the rest of the world. And when that happens, you'd crave for any attention from other interesting people just to feel better about yourself and your ability to communicate.

How Can I Stay in Love Forever?

This is the biggest problem in a relationship, and one that's hardest to overcome. Falling in love is easy. Staying in love isn't. Love is a delicate balance between dependency and passion. How much do you need your partner? How much do you love and want your partner? When the sexual excitement and the enthusiasm fade away, what do you have to hold both of you together? A relationship should never be based on sex alone. It needs compatibility and understanding, and it definitely needs dependability. Staying in love forever is not easy, but with a little effort, it can give meaning to your life.

How Can an Unmet Emotional Need Lead to Relationship Problems?

A close relationship between the couple provides an ideal opportunity for many of the essential emotional needs of both partners to be met. Meanwhile, relationship problems can occur when one or both parties feel that their needs are not being met. A marriage or partnership can also become troubled if you either misuse or do not maximise your natural resources, and you are not taking care of your emotional needs. This can lead you to become unhappy and to suffer with emotional, mental, and social problems.

Can We Expect All of Our Needs to Be Met in Our Relationship or Marriage?

Being overly dependent on each other often leads to relationship or marriage problems too. Please note that if you feel that your needs aren't being met, it is a warning sign—not a *green light* for infidelity! Unrealistic expectations can lead to disappointment and resentment. However, your view of precisely what is classed as *realistic* is likely to be different from mine and from your partner's. Therein lies the problem, as well as the solution. By looking at your perception of the problems and your reactions, rather than blaming your partner, you're more likely to make the right decisions about how to overcome the difficulties.

Managing Conflict

It's time to stop avoiding conflict and instead look for ways to deal with conflict more effectively. As analysed by speaker, Les Brown, *"Don't be afraid of conflict; abandon the concept of winning and losing when faced with conflict; try using positive language that disarms rather than confronts; like and find something to distract you from the conflict."*

Practical Ways to Keep the Fire of Love Burning

There are ways to keep romance in your marriage and to keep the fire of love burning. Below are suggestions, but you need to find and use your spouse's love language. What do they like? What communicates to them better that you love them? Do these things regularly. The little things on a daily basis make a significant difference.

Call your spouse by a pet name. Allow the man to exercise his authority as the head of the family, and let the woman be the heart. Let the husband honour his wife, and the wife admire her husband. Respect each other. Appreciate each other. Speak well of your spouse before their friends and siblings. Praise them before your children. Smile when you look at them, and give them occasional pecks when you are out socially. Honour their mother. Insist that they buy gifts for their parents, and be sure that they will do the same for your parents. Surprise them with their favourite things.

Give them a warm reception with an embrace when they return from work or from an outing, and help undress them. Put love notes in their lunch box, briefcase, or bag. Phone and tell them that you love them or are missing them. Tell them how blessed you are to have them. Hug them for no reason.

Remember, be quick to say, "I'm sorry dear," and be quick to forgive. Always pray for them, and pray together often.

Finally...

TAKE TIME

Take time to think; it is the source of power.
Take time to play; it is the secret of perpetual youth.
Take time to read; it is the fountain of wisdom.
Take time to pray; it is the greatest power on earth.

Take time to love and be loved; it is a God-given privilege.
Take time to be friendly; it is the road to happiness.
Take time to laugh; it is the music of the soul and medicine to the heart.
Take time to give; it is too short a day to be selfish.
Take time to forgive; it is a way of freedom.
Take time to work; it is the price of success.
Take time to do charity; it is the key to heaven.

TESTIMONIALS

"Do you want to learn from the best? A person who tells you what to do, or a person who is doing it and speaks from their experience? That is why any person, committed to reaching the best version the Creator wants them to be, would benefit from reading *Yes, You Can*. Elizabeth Lucas-Afolalu speaks from a commitment to scripture, and a wealth of experience, with a message that grips the heart. Penetrating, yet practical, it beckons everyone to boldly embrace the call to action as a witness of the power of God. This book brings a fresh perspective to the greatest mission of all. The world needs this message, and every person needs this book."
Eduardo Sena, Entrepreneur, Bob Proctor Consultant, International Speaker and Author, *Unstoppable*.

"A fantastic book. It not only gives hope but offers practical solutions, and points you in the right direction to seek God for yourself and for your situations."
Eniola Alabi, founder, Apples of Gold Creative Communications.

"Elizabeth is a determined woman. Throughout her experiences and hardships, she managed to find her balance to be able to solve her problems. Because of her ventures, she was able to garner the knowledge that she needs to write a book that will surely inspire millions of people from all around the world."
Eduardo Sena, Entrepreneur, Bob Proctor Consultant, International Speaker and Author, *Unstoppable*.

ABOUT THE AUTHOR

Elizabeth Lucas-Afolalu's passions are outreach, and supporting women, young married couples, and young adults. Her interests inventory and work values assessment confirm her passions. Her personality assessment shows a God loving, compassionate and very thorough person. She believes in relationships, families, friendship, success, and prayer. She regularly enjoys visiting people, inspiring, motivating, coaching, mentoring, and giving support where needed. She is also a creative, industrious, and hard-working woman. She is married, with two lovely children.

As an award-winning, inspirational, and transformational speaker, writer, and entrepreneur extraordinaire, her passion for business led her to obtain an honours degree in business and management at the University of Northampton, United Kingdom. She was awarded Secretary of the Year, by Brook Street Bureau and Lewisham College, in England. Elizabeth has worked with other organisations as administrator, secretary, and personal assistant, and has worked in various sectors, such as Local Government Management Board, City and Guilds, Tower Hamlet Consortium, Environment Agency, Central Family Court, and the NHS. She is actively involved with NGO charities such as Jesus Fellowship, CFAN, Aofac Foundation, Elderly People with Dementia, British Heart Foundation, British Dementia Befriending Foundation, Alzheimer's Society, UK Compassion, Great Ormond Street Hospital for Children, National Deaf Children Association, and Salvation Army Homeless Unit. Her work has involved reaching out to ex-prisoners and drug addicts. She is the managing director of Elizabeth Kreations Limited, and director of Tokmez Limited, both in the UK. She is the UK Chief Bureau Editor of an American magazine, *Okuns Group Magazine*, and the exceptional author of *Yes, You Can.*

Do you think you could become, be,
and do much more than you are doing now?

Do you need motivation and help to develop perseverance to
pursue your life goals?

Do you want to develop the mindset that will push you
to improve your character traits, which will lead you to
unlimited success in life?

Do you want to have a healthy relationship and be happy?

Perhaps, you are not showing up as much as you know you should.

Or you suffer worry and anxiety about being visible
on social media, in person, or anywhere else.

Or you need help to overcome low self-esteem
and lack of confidence. And you want support to step into your
power show up and show off.

I have created something very special to help you. I offer 30
minutes free consultation of Yes, You Can Life Coaching in areas of
Relationship, Empowerment, Personal Development, and Success.

I have six years of experience of mentoring individuals and families
ascribing for success, and there are positive results and
testimonies, including my life experience, which I have uploaded
and downloaded into a system.

Visit www.yesyoucan-by-elizabeth.com

ELIZABETH KREATIONS –
INSPIRATIONAL AND MOTIVATIONAL GIFTS FOR ALL

A collection of inspirational and motivational gifts and resources that give us the courage to pursue our life's dreams and goals, and that have the power to even get us through a bad week.

Our gift shop is known for providing highly inspiring, innovative, and humorous gifts, stylish home décor, and desirable collectables. You can also have your item personalised for that special person or for yourself.

We have an excellent collection of highly inspirational stories, articles, videos, and other materials that leave you deeply inspired to be all that you can be, and all are available to order from our website. Creating a library of inspirational resources is a vital way to increase your spiritual growth and have valuable insight into God's Word.

Available items include:

inspirational greeting cards, inspirational posters, inspirational frames, inspirational plaques, inspirational handkerchiefs, hand and face towels, inspirational T-shirts, polos, caps, and sweatshirts, inspirational Mugs, inspirational coasters, inspirational magnets, inspirational badges, inspirational key rings, inspirational teddies, inspirational canvas, inspirational bookmarks, inspirational bracelets.

Visit: www.elizabethkreations.co.uk